Geometric Designs and Patterns

COLOR TEST

TEST YOUR COLOR SUPPLIES ON THIS PAGE TO SEE HOW THEY REACT TO THE PAPER.

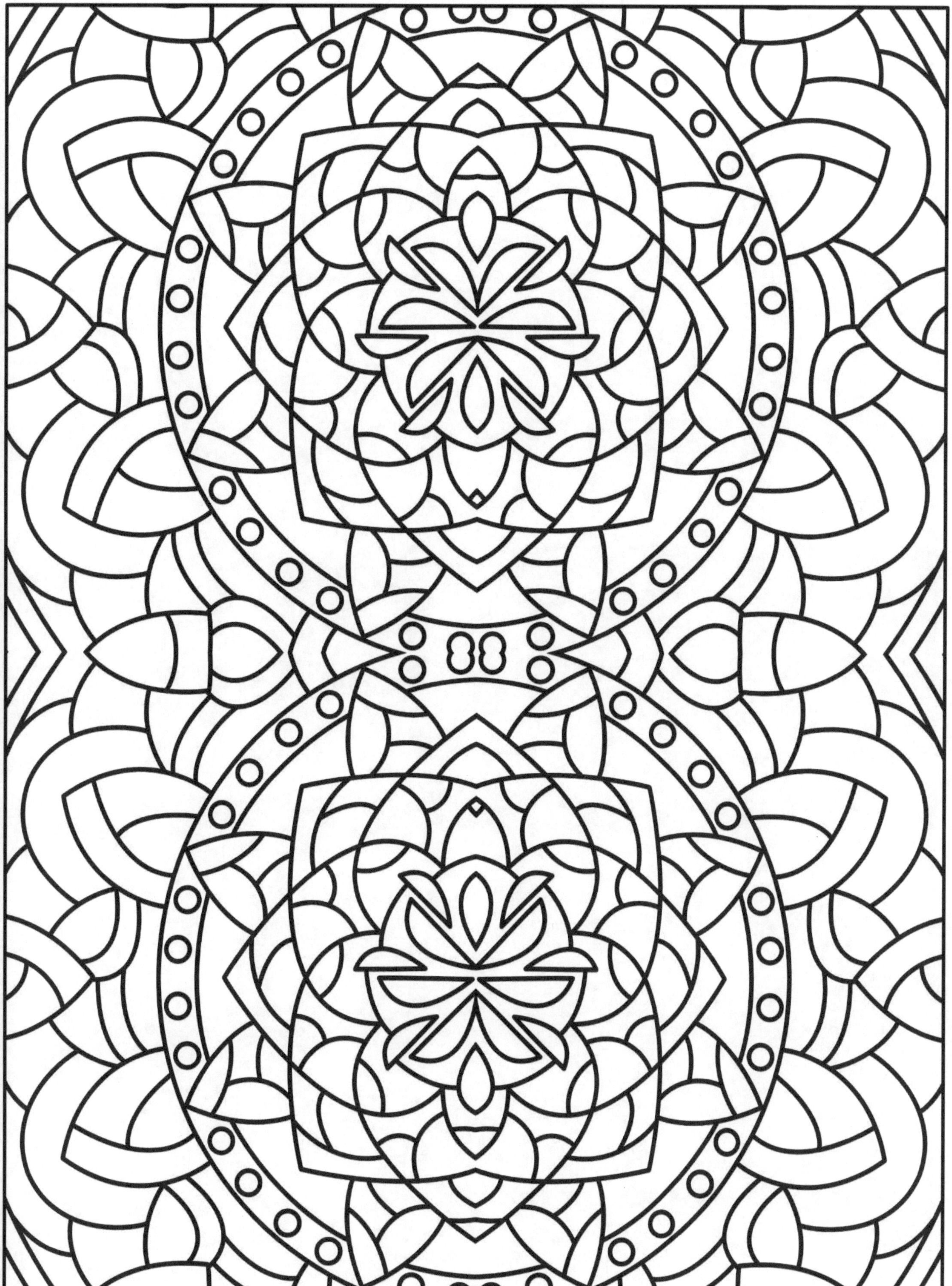

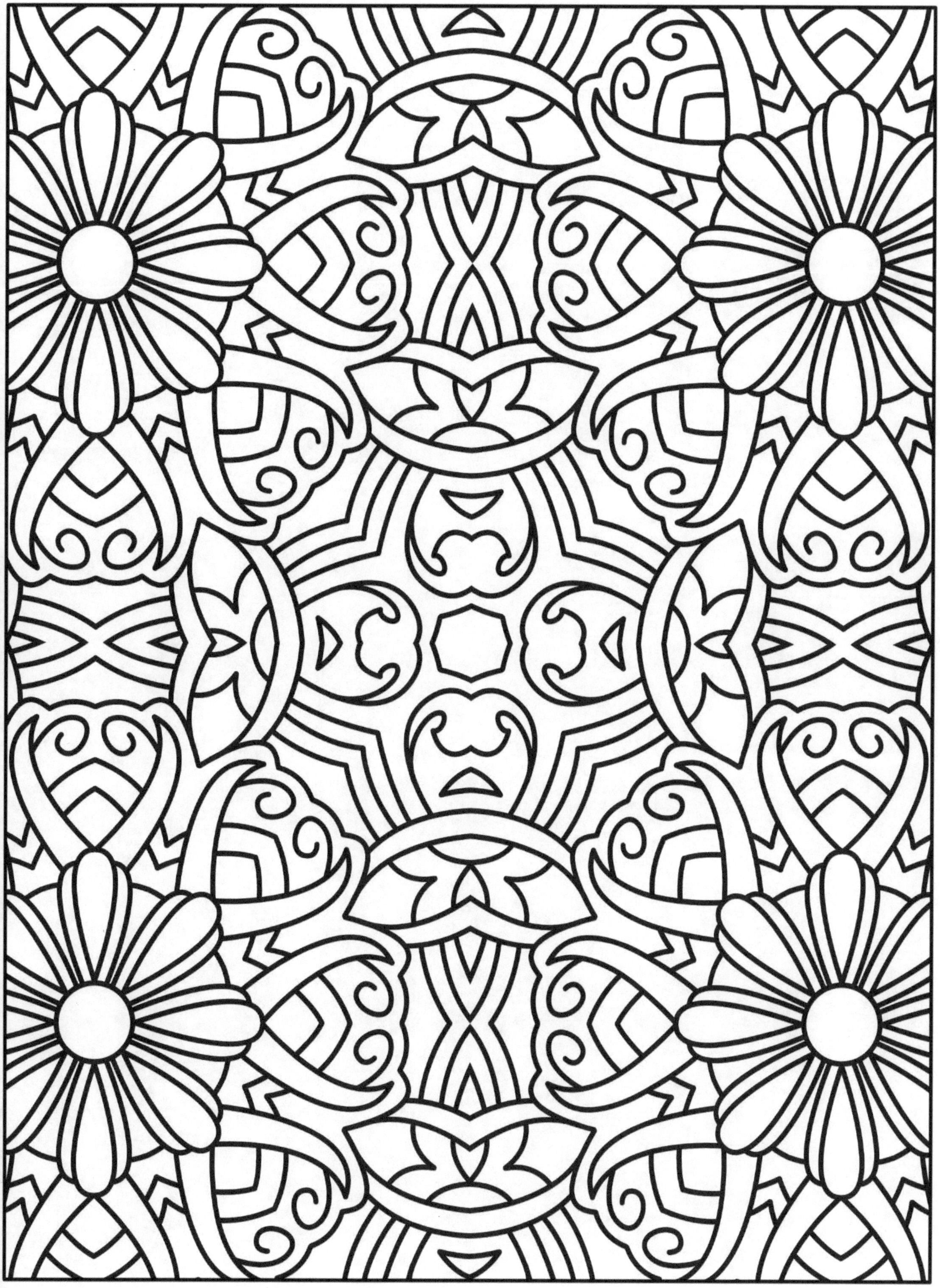

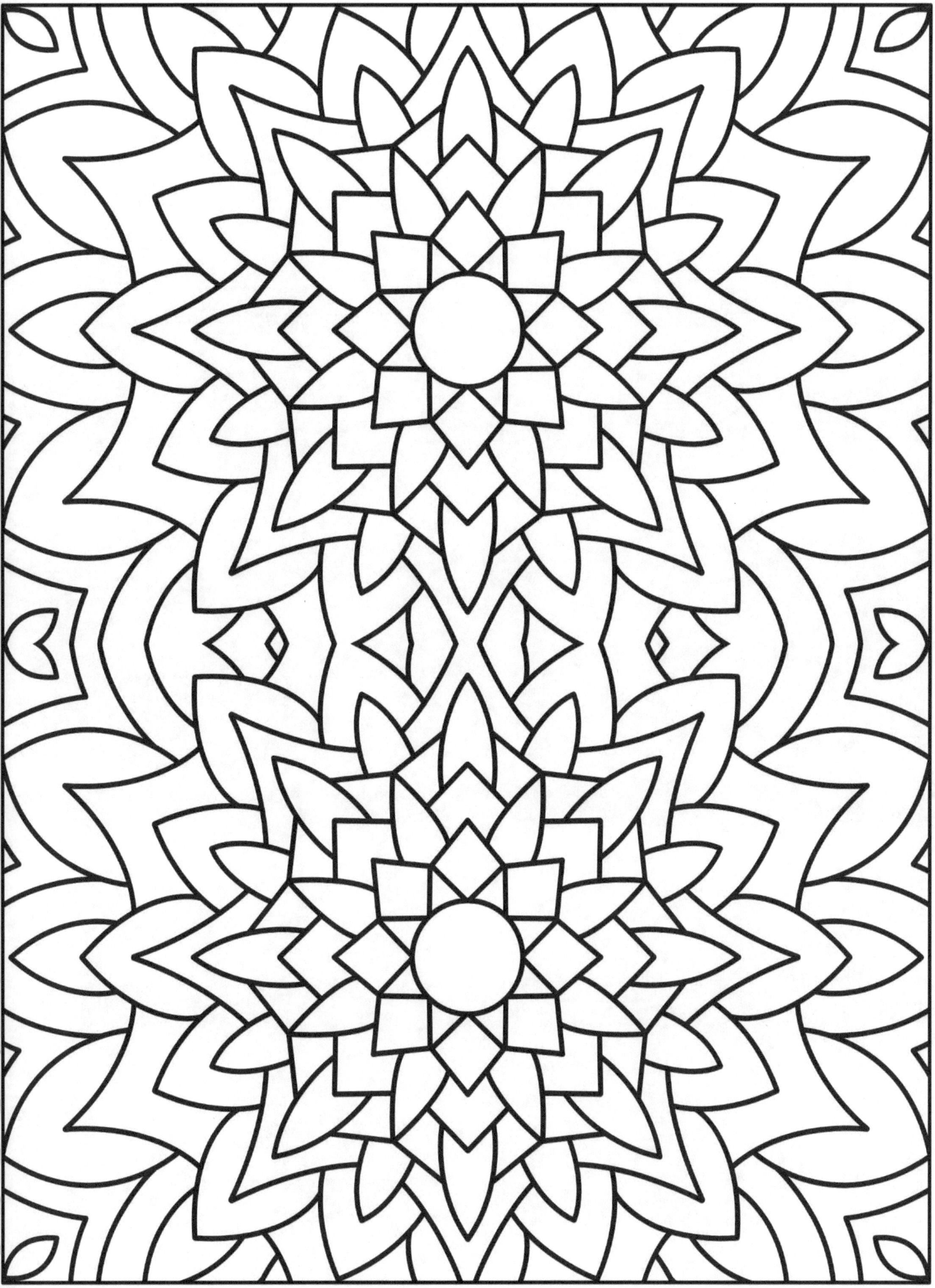

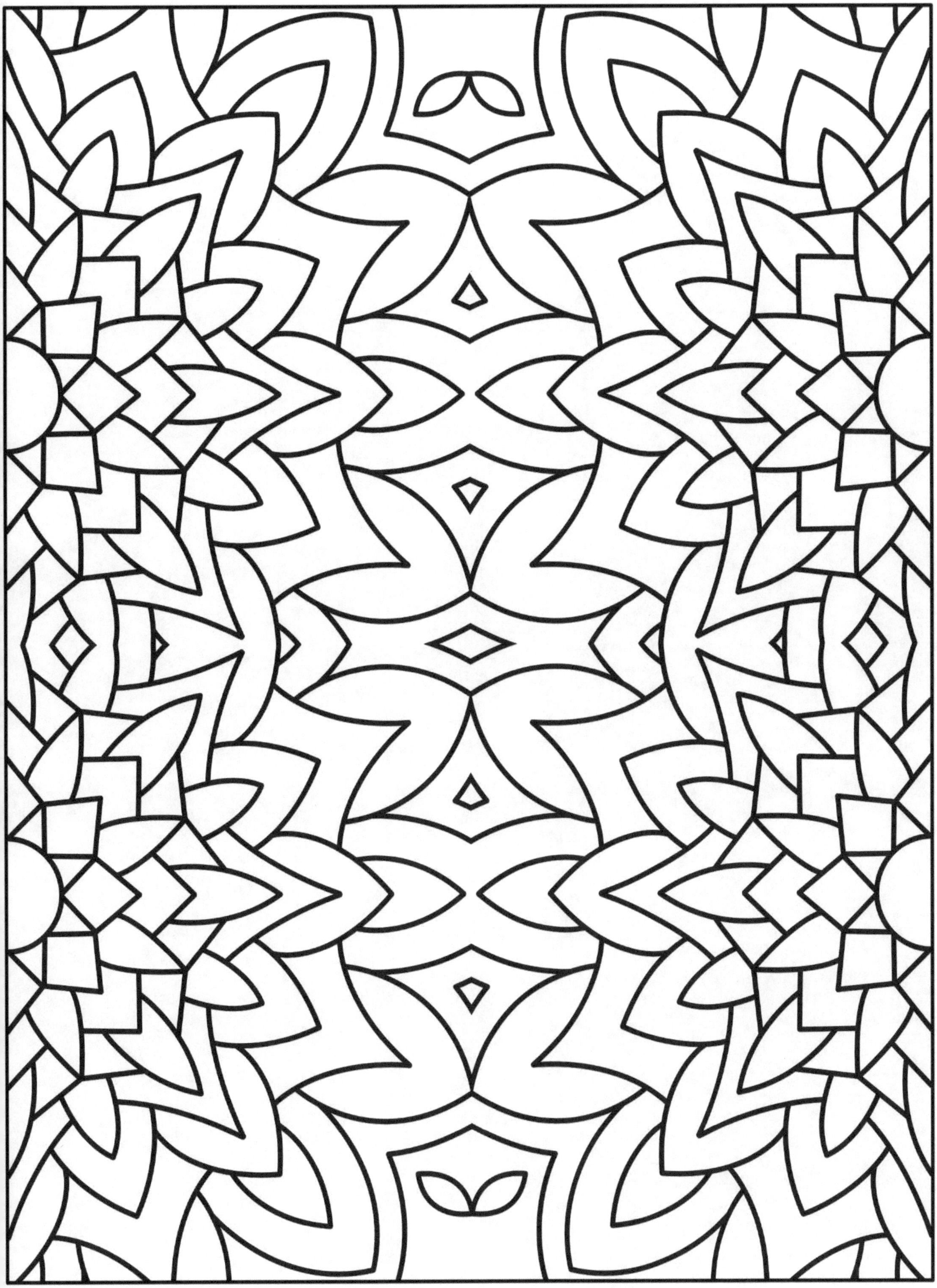

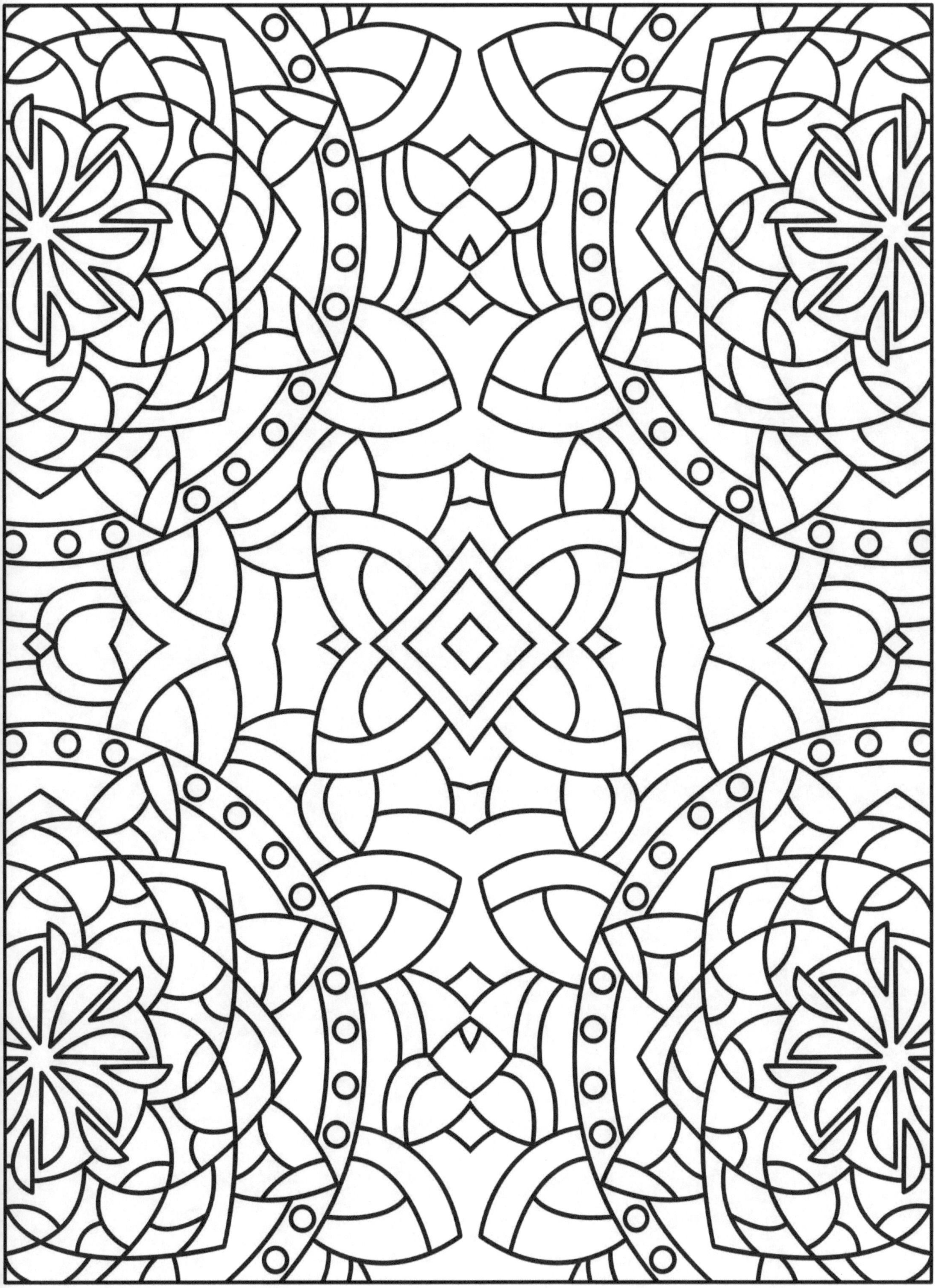

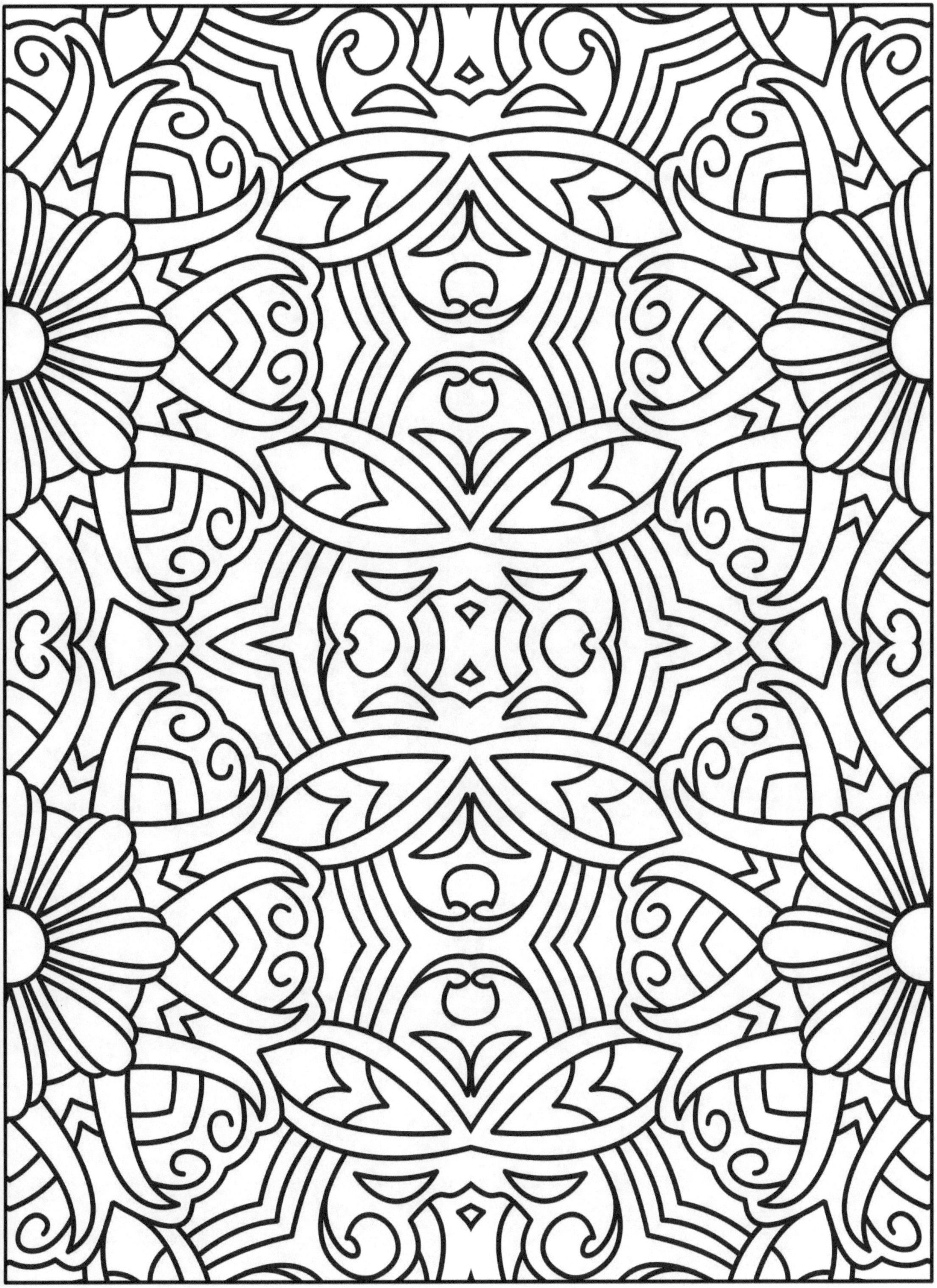

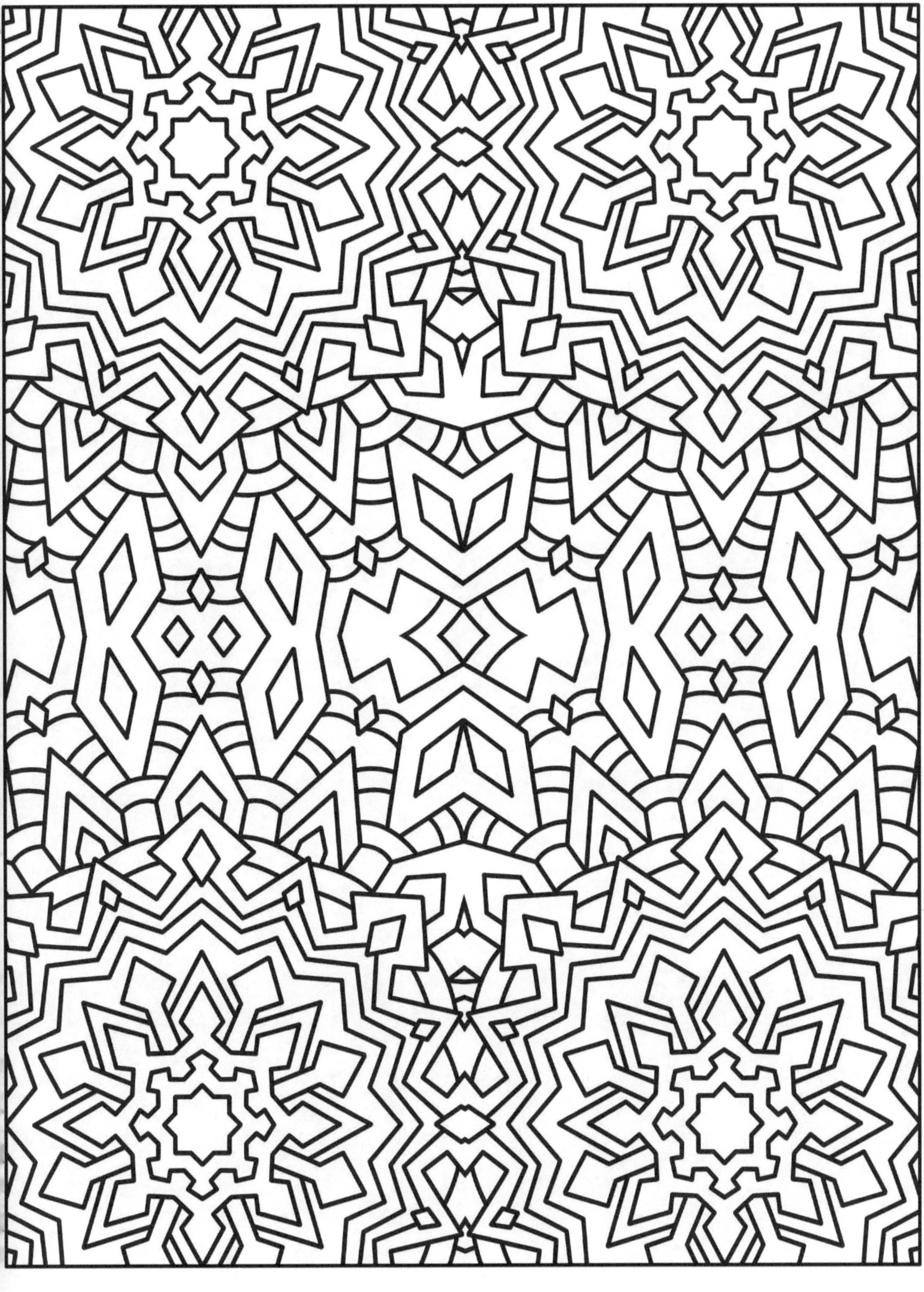

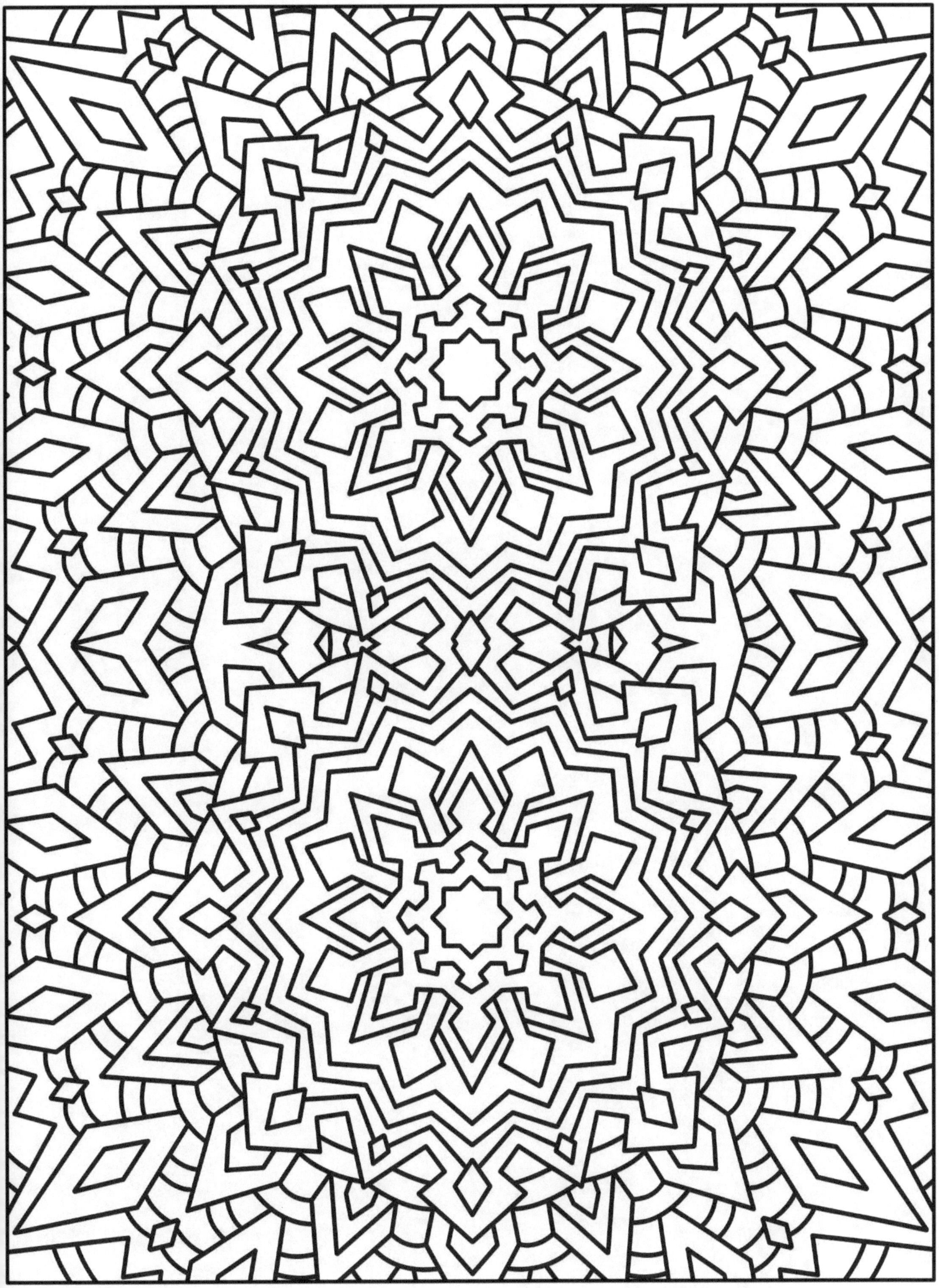

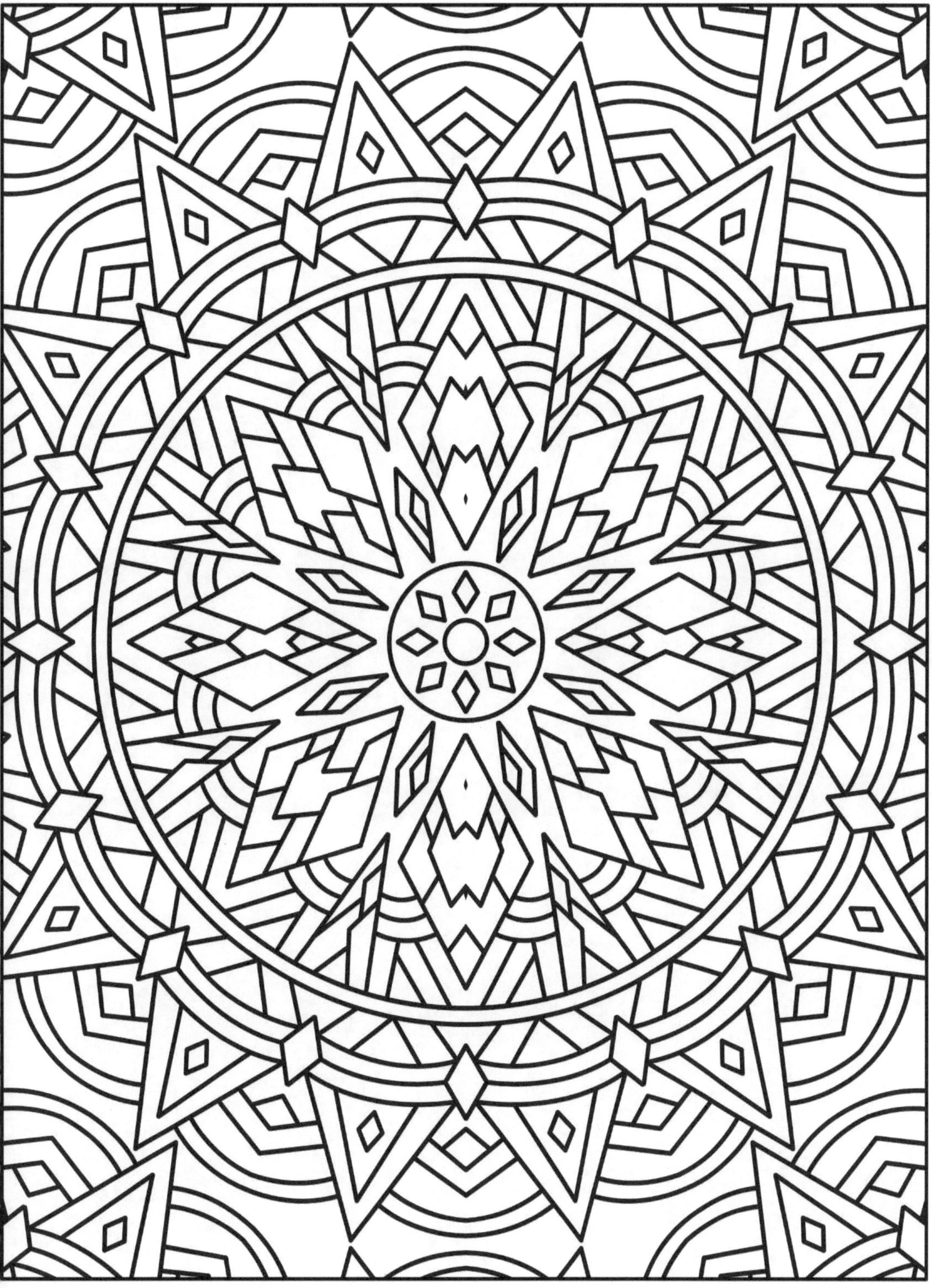

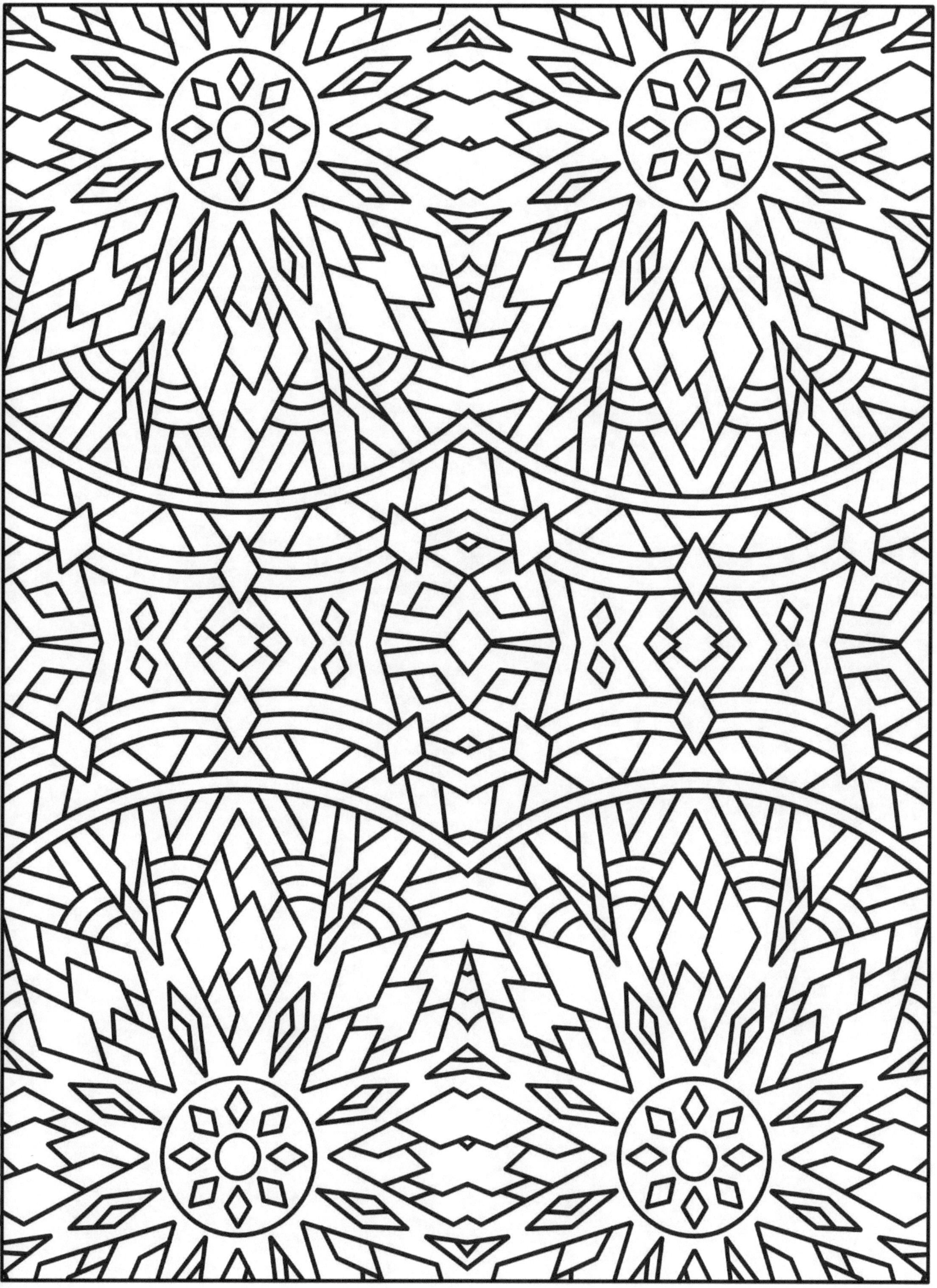

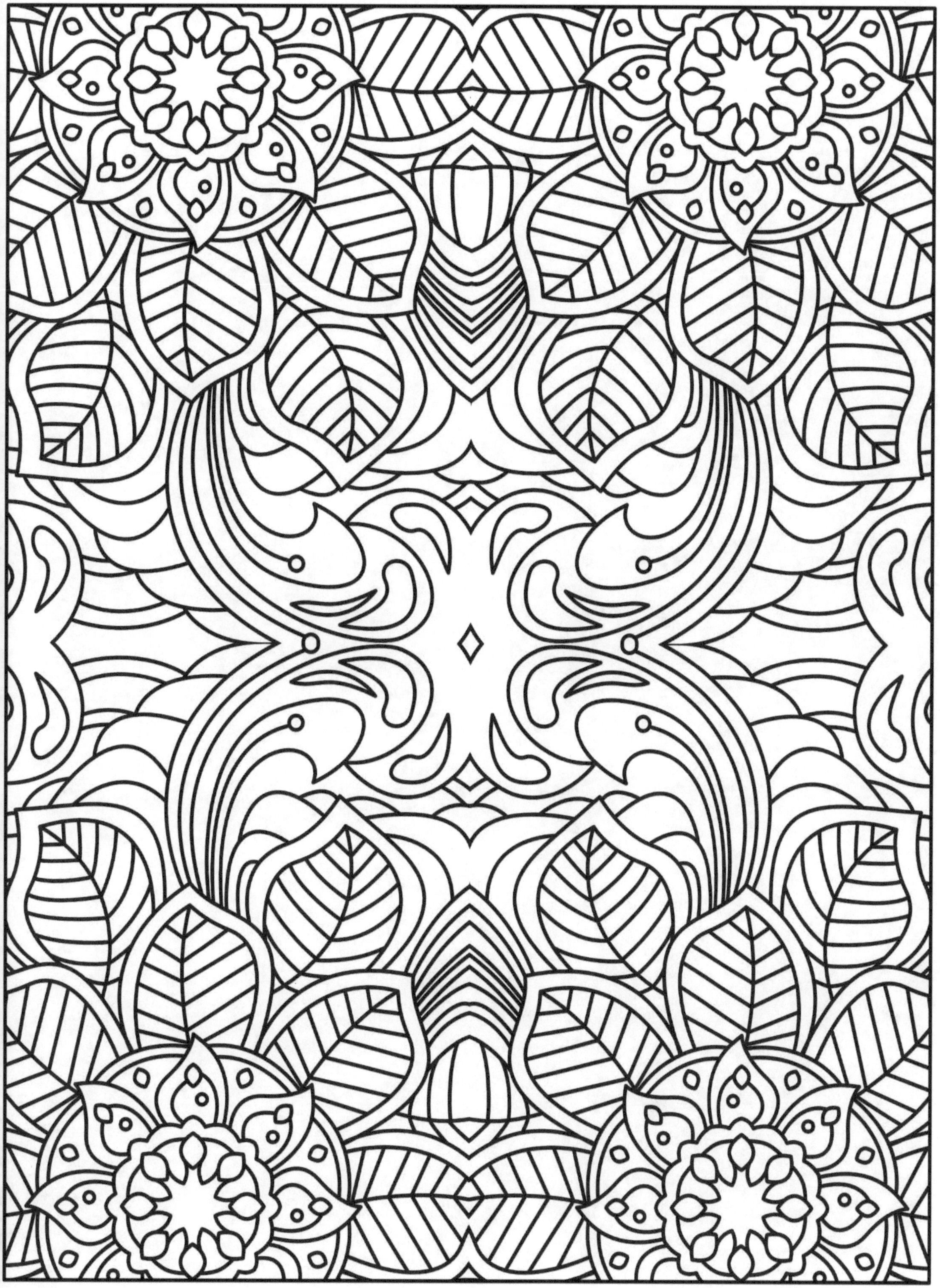

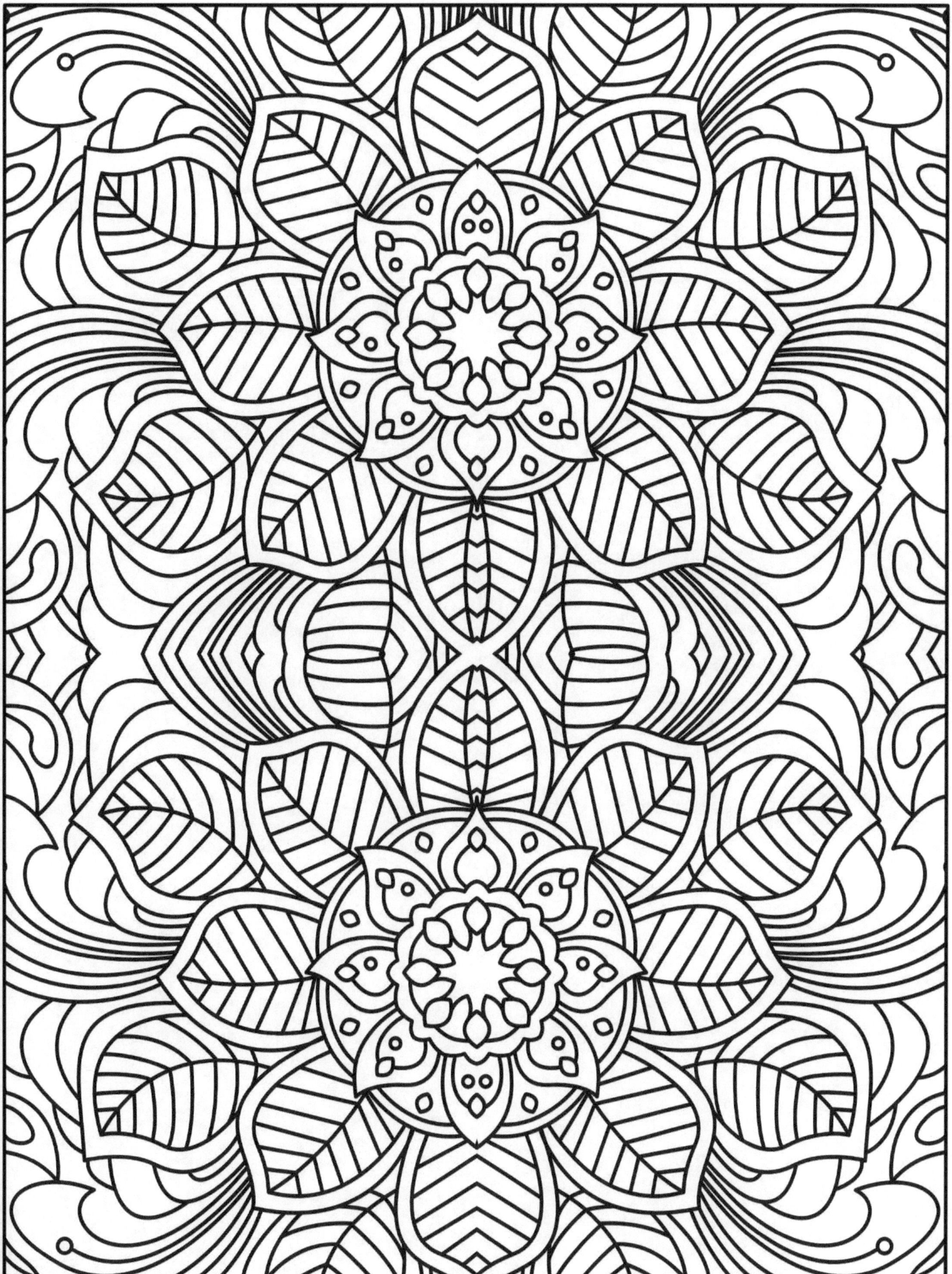

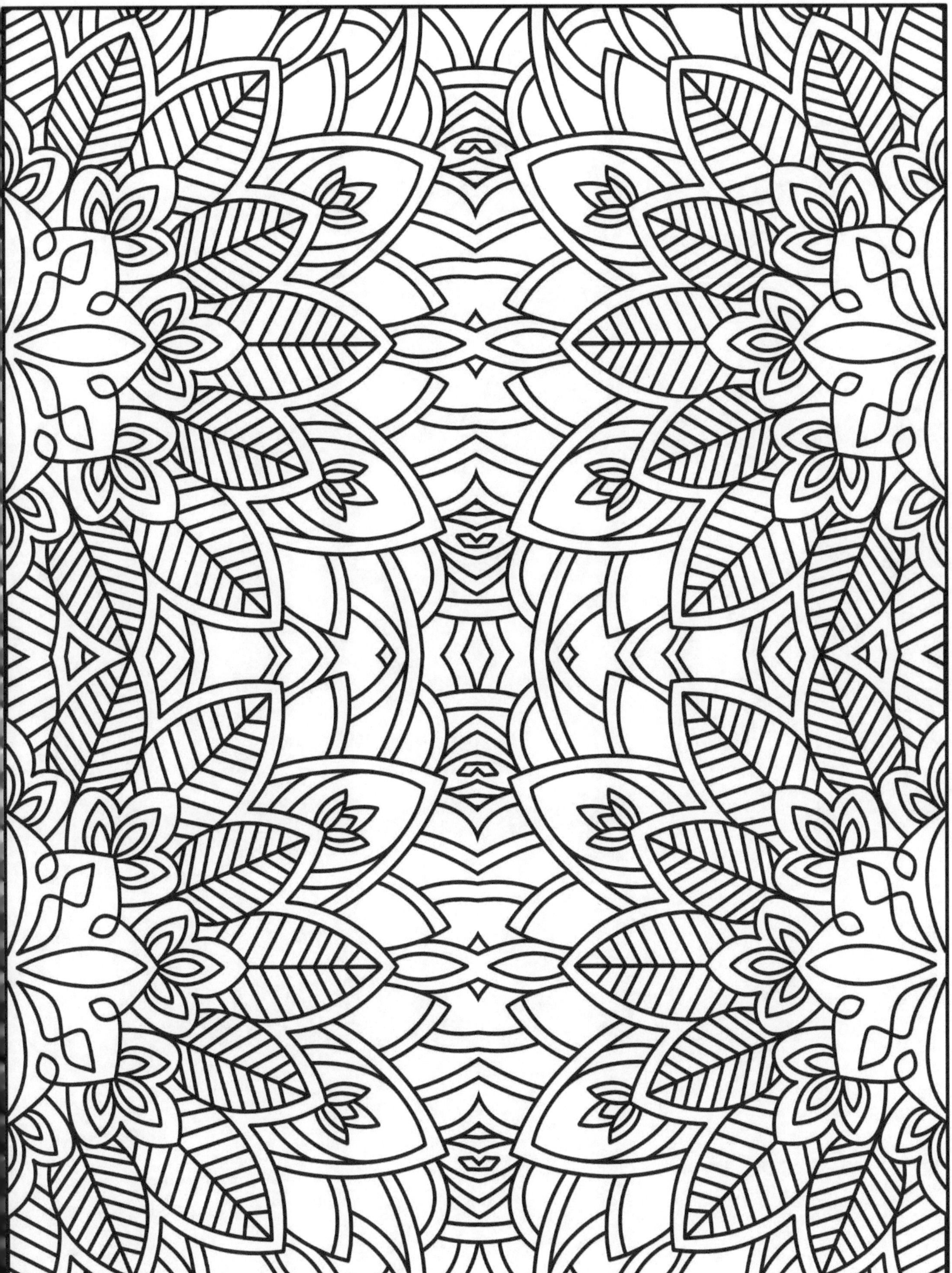

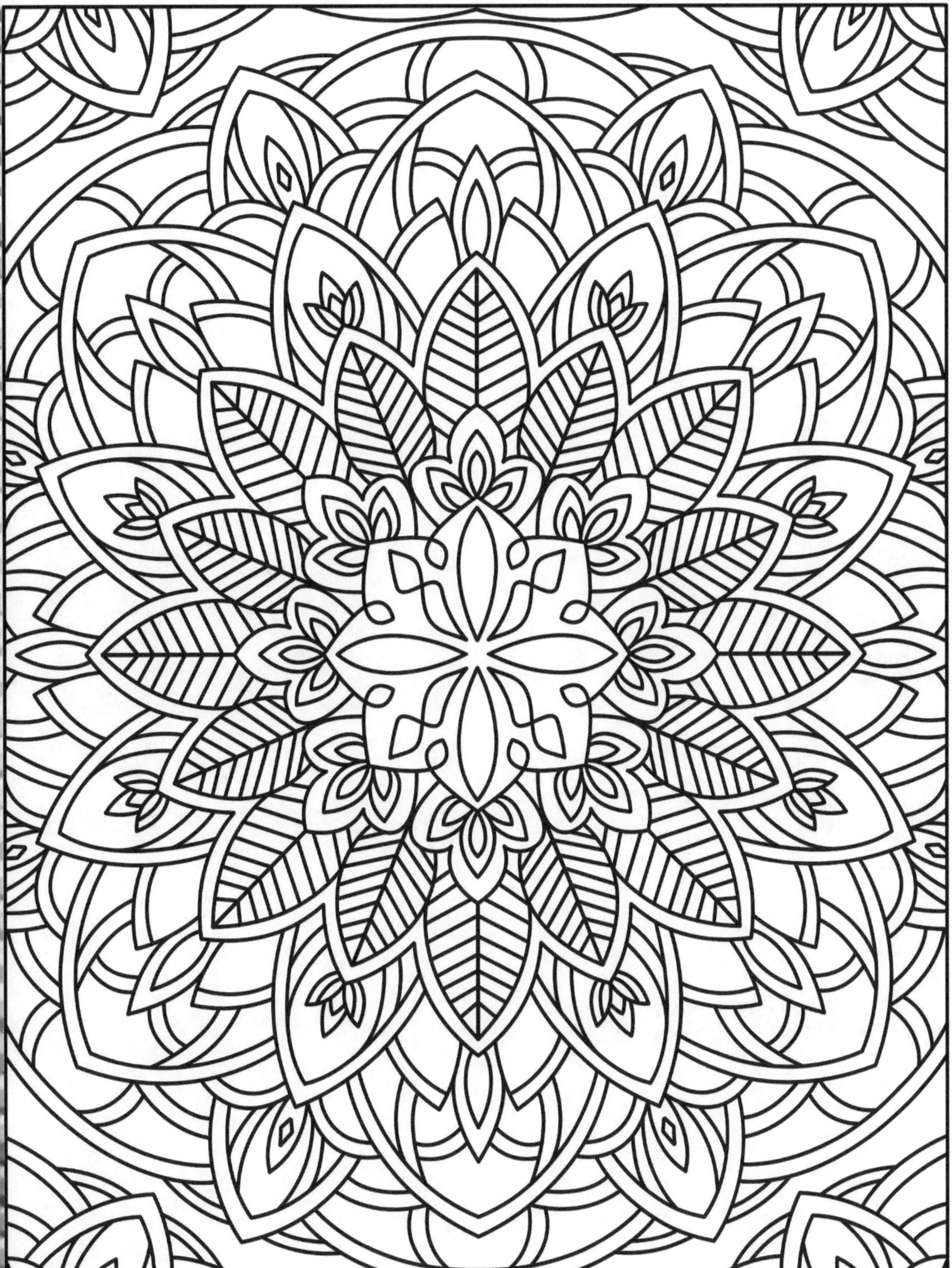

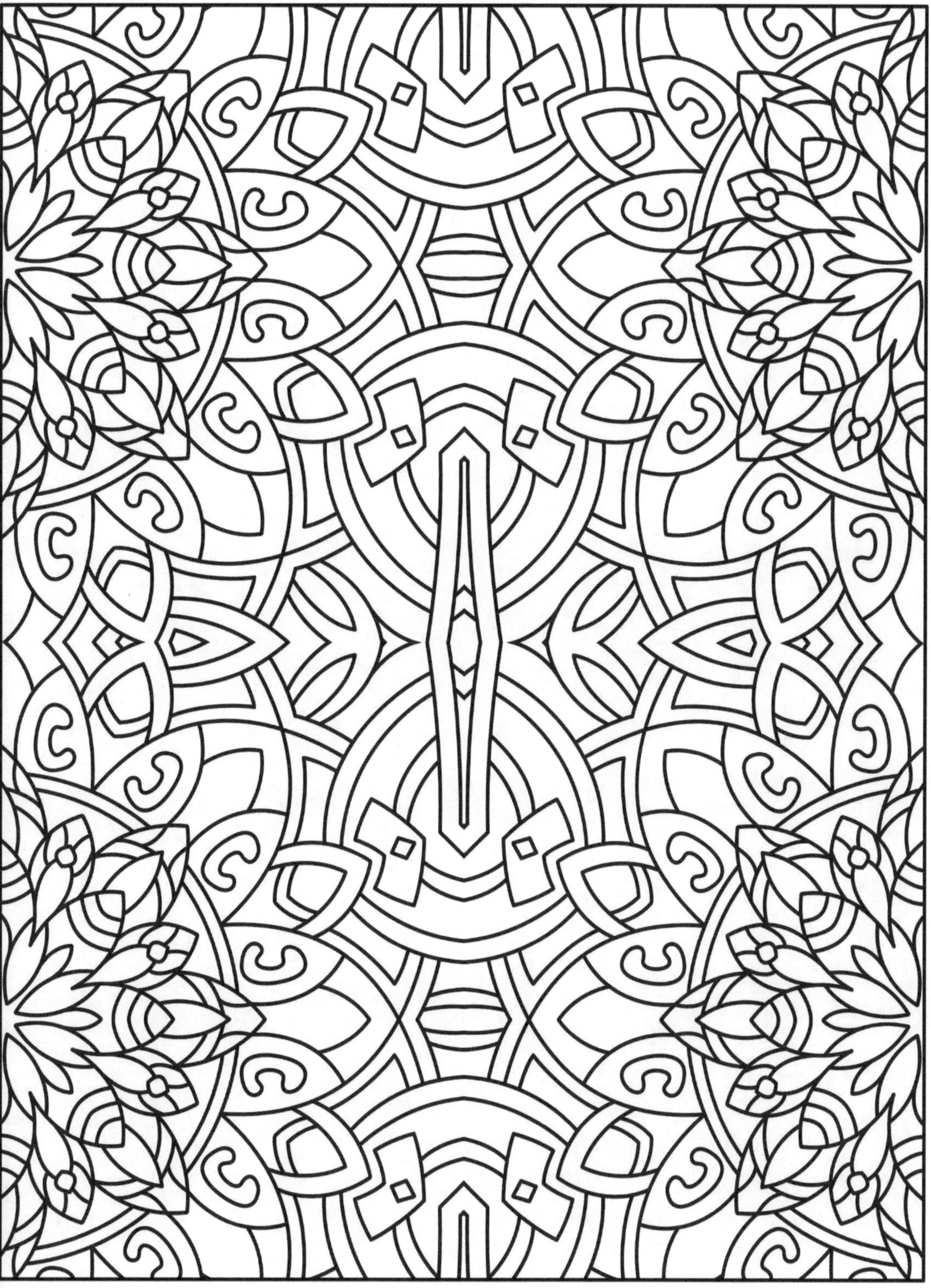

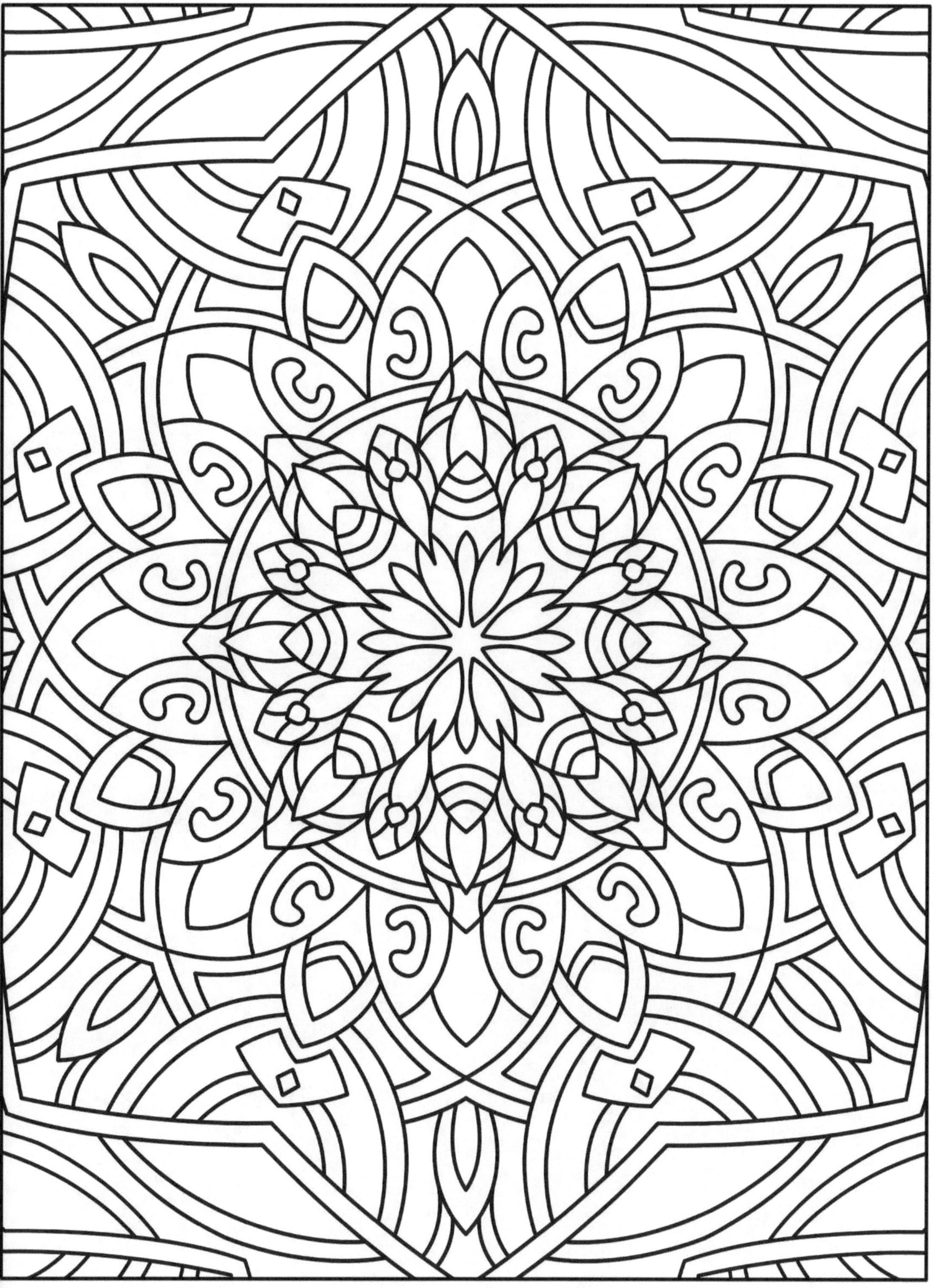

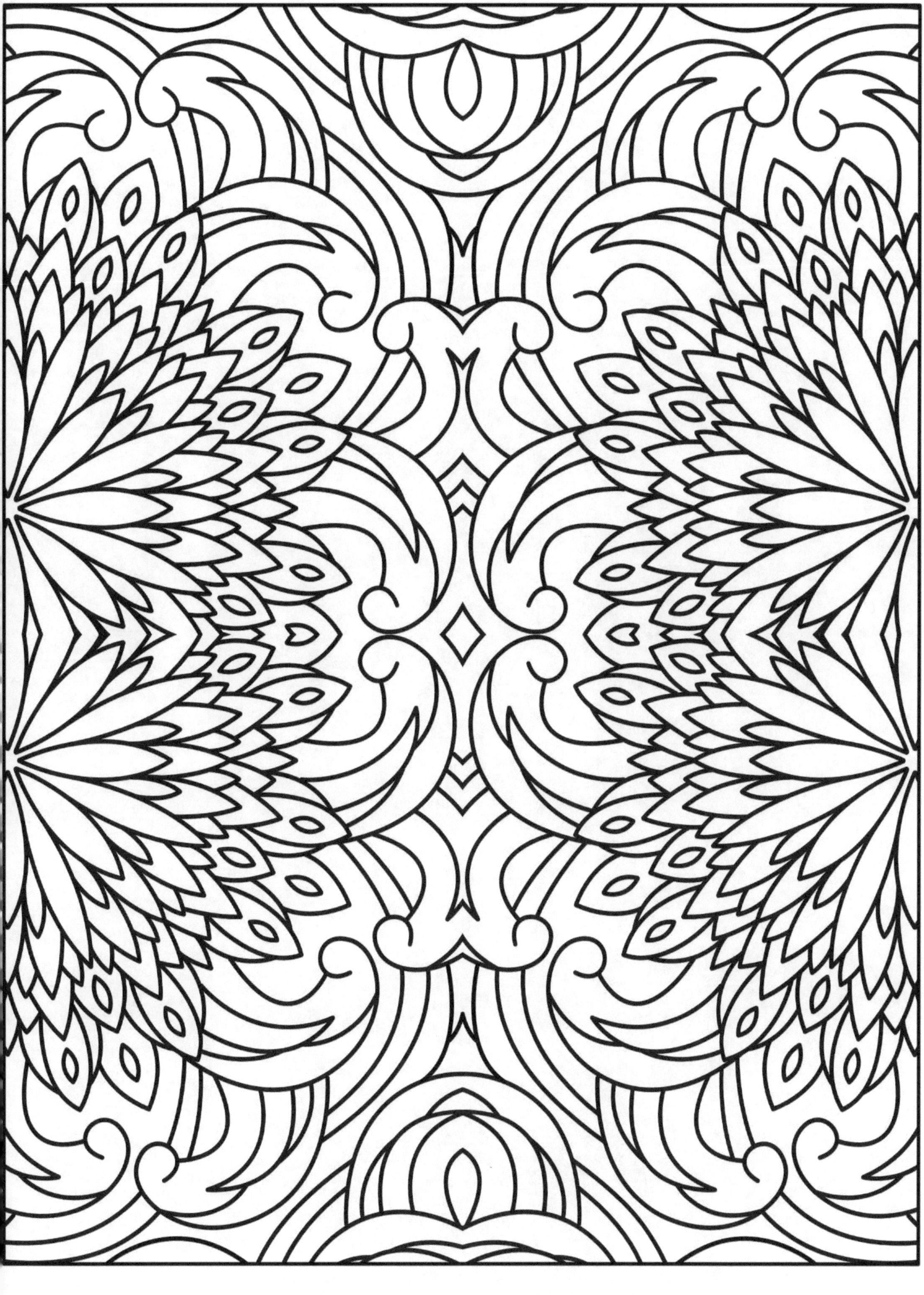

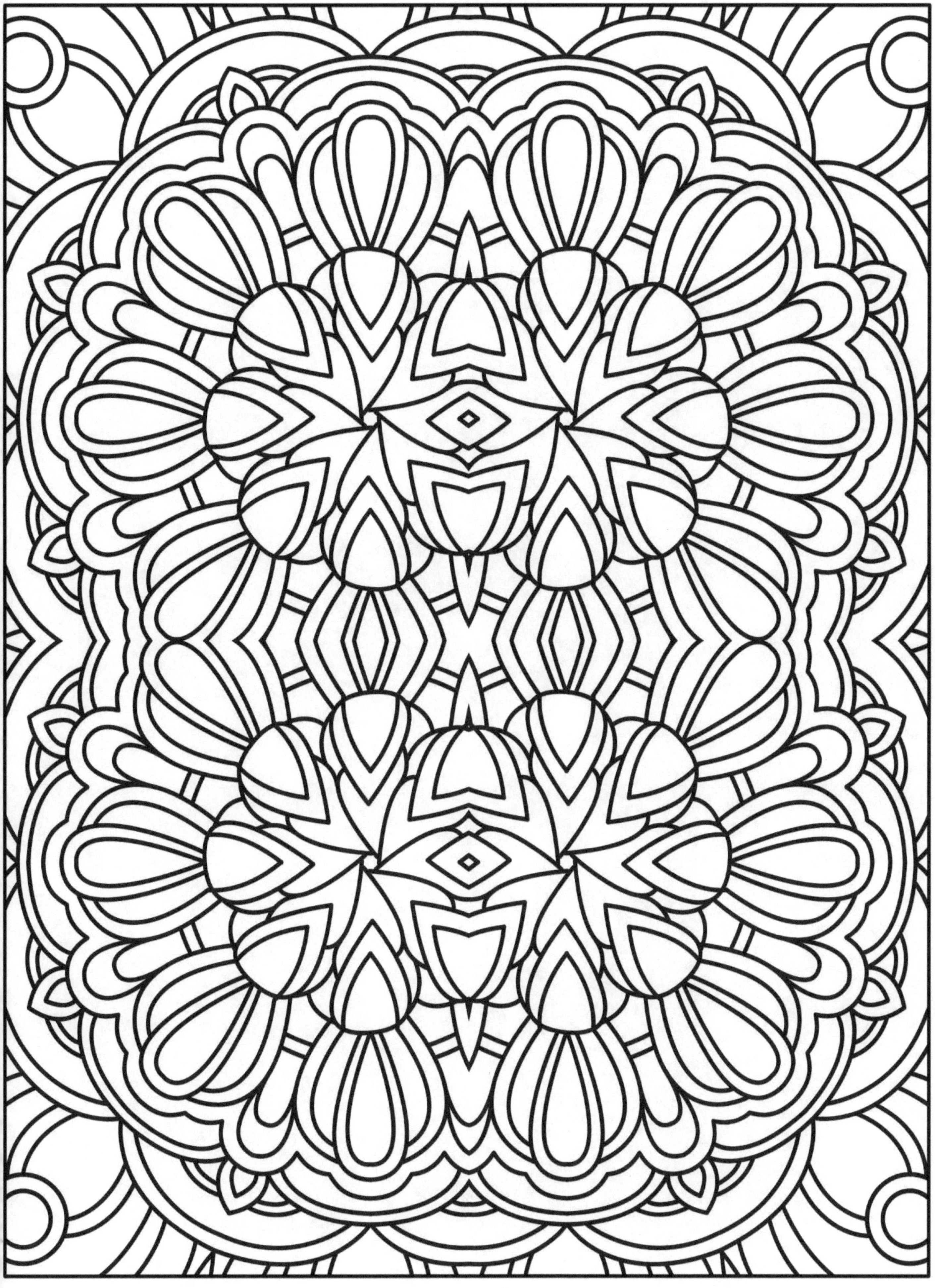

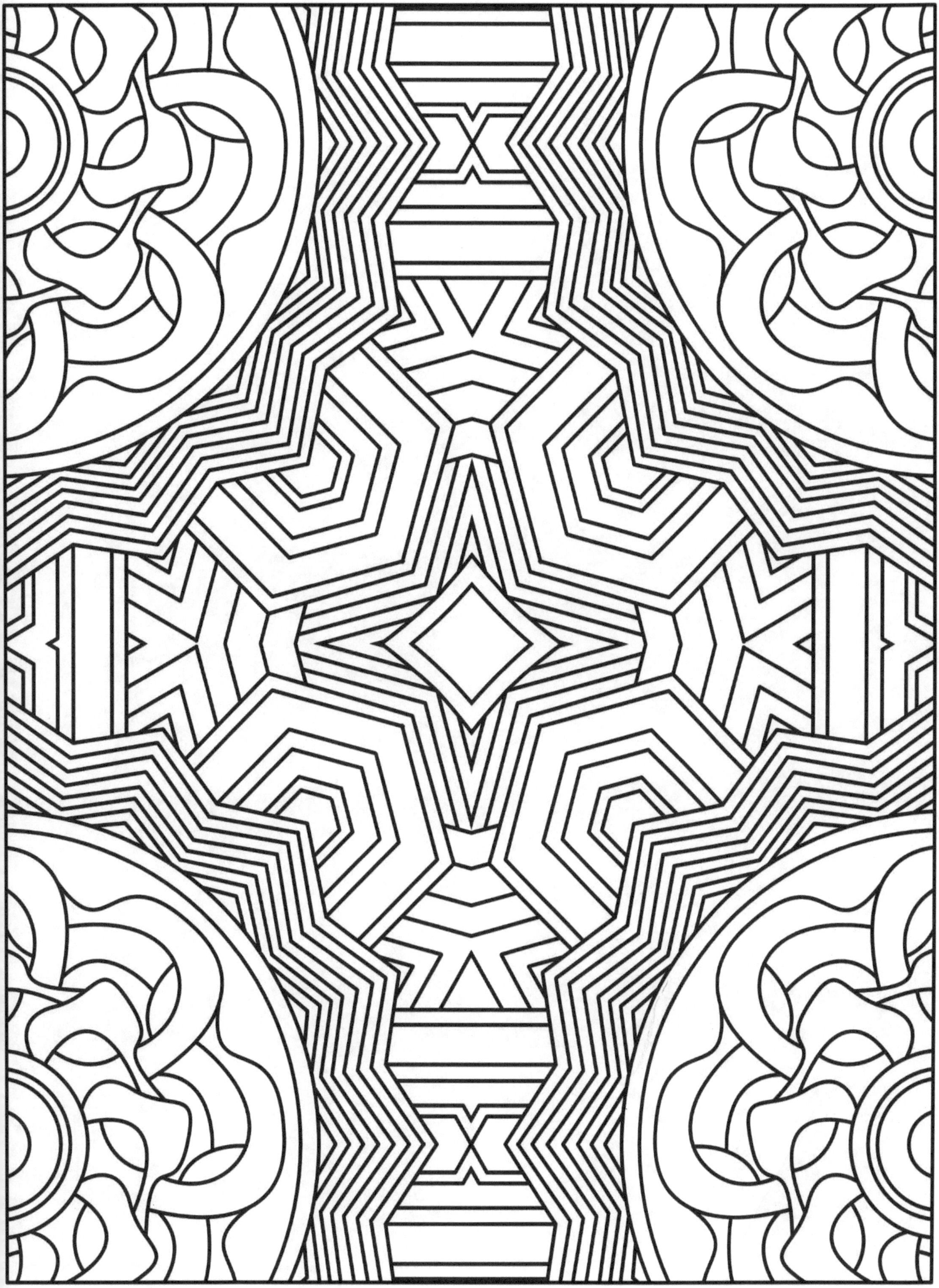

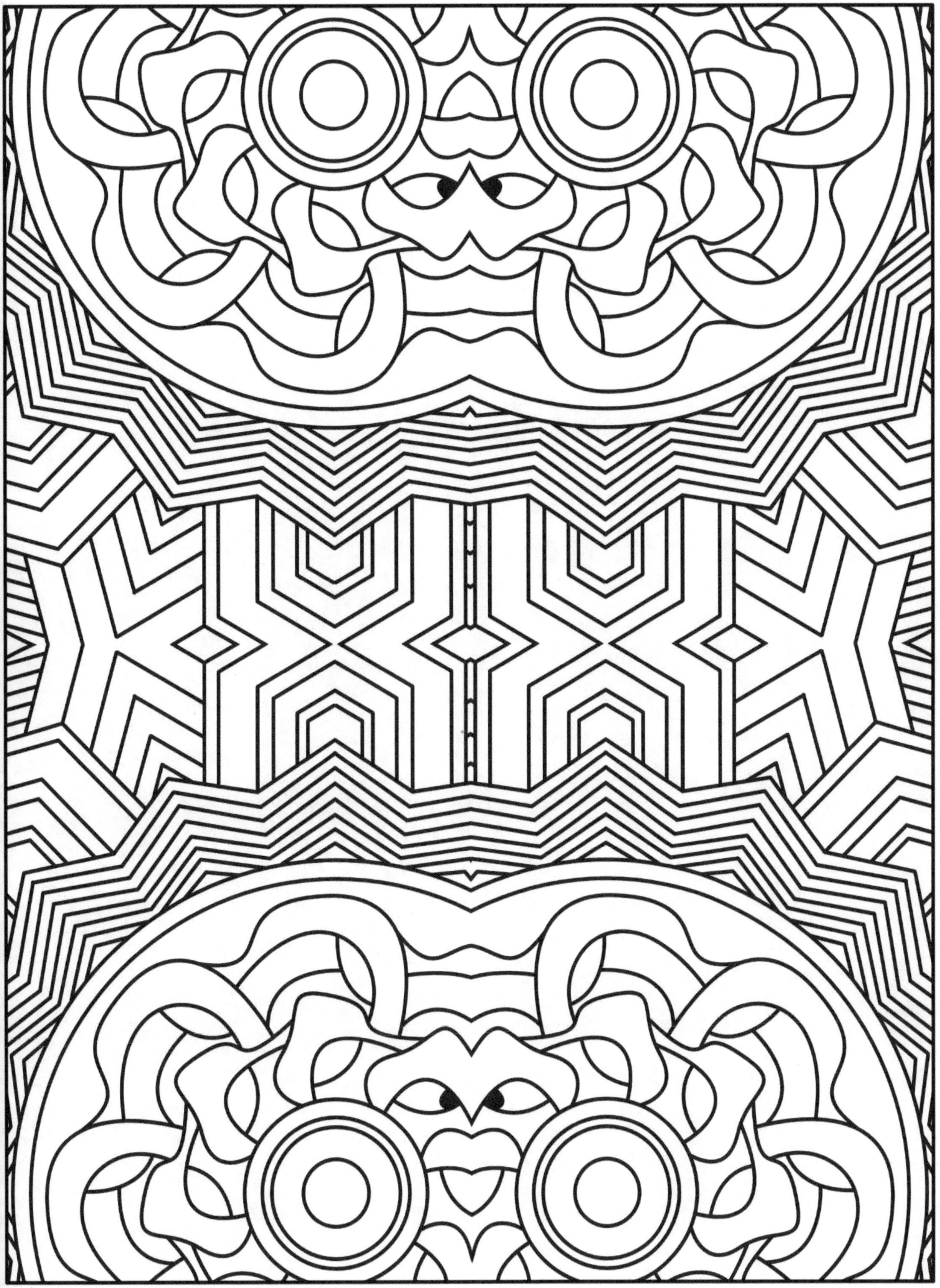

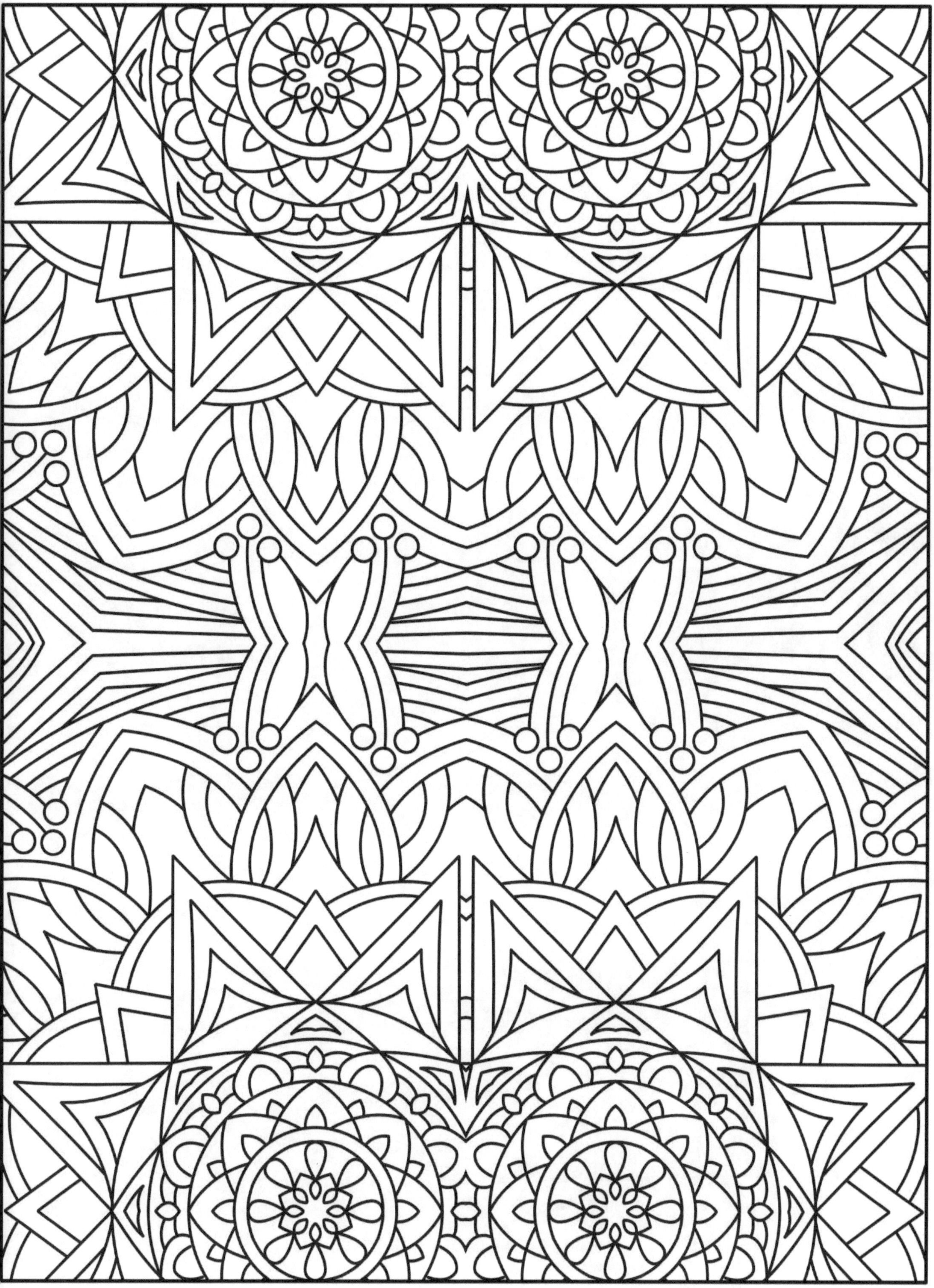

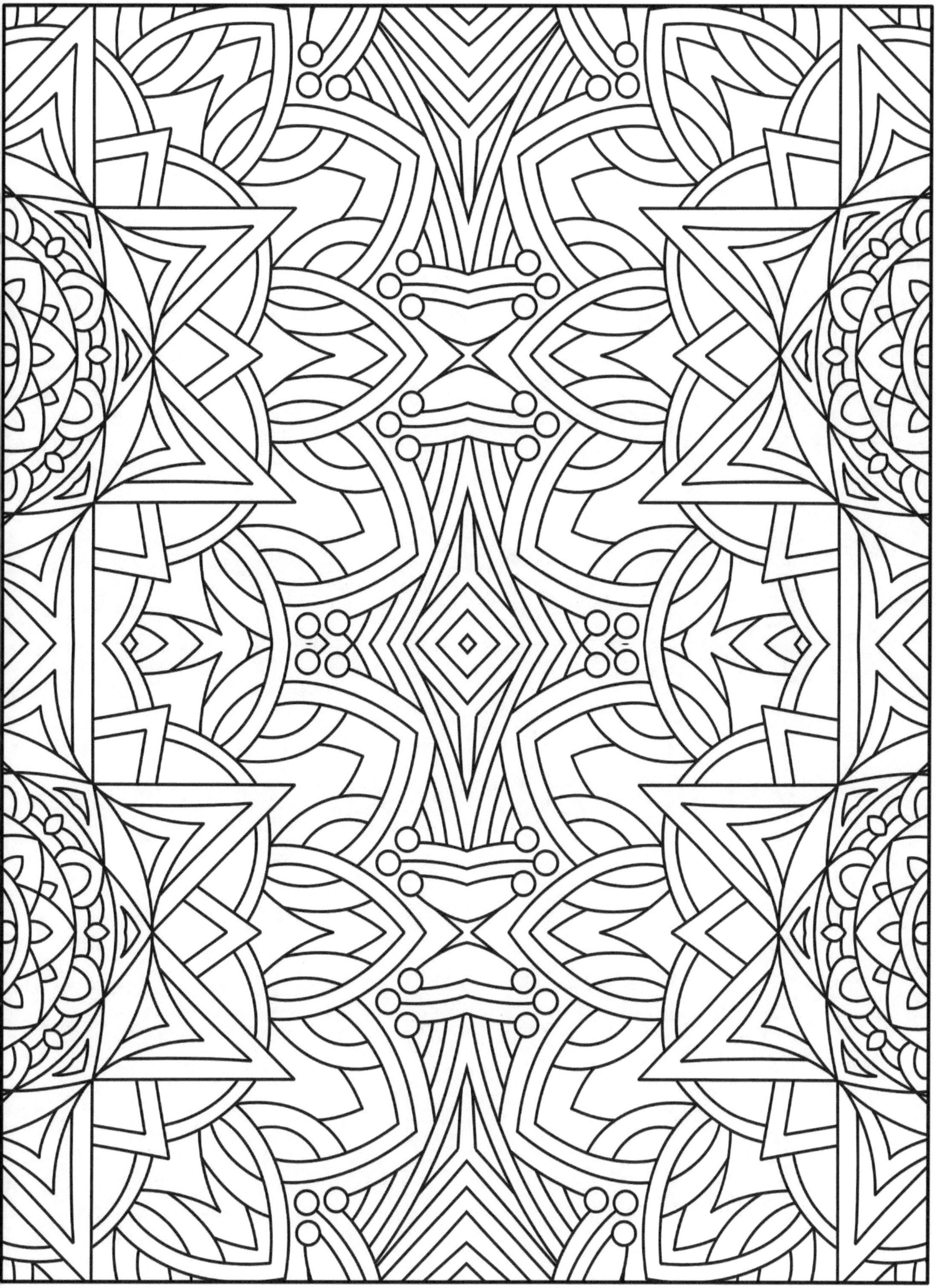

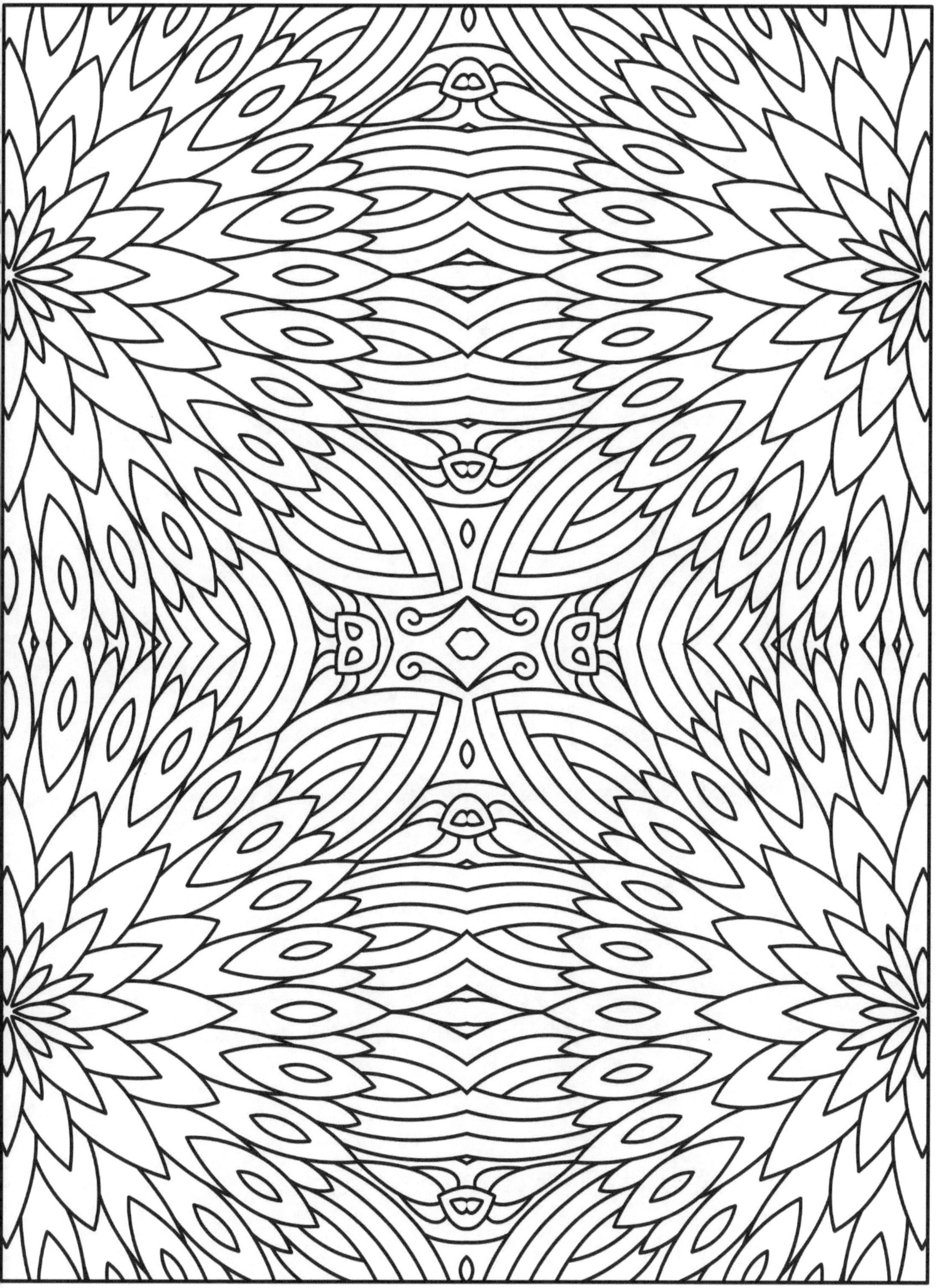

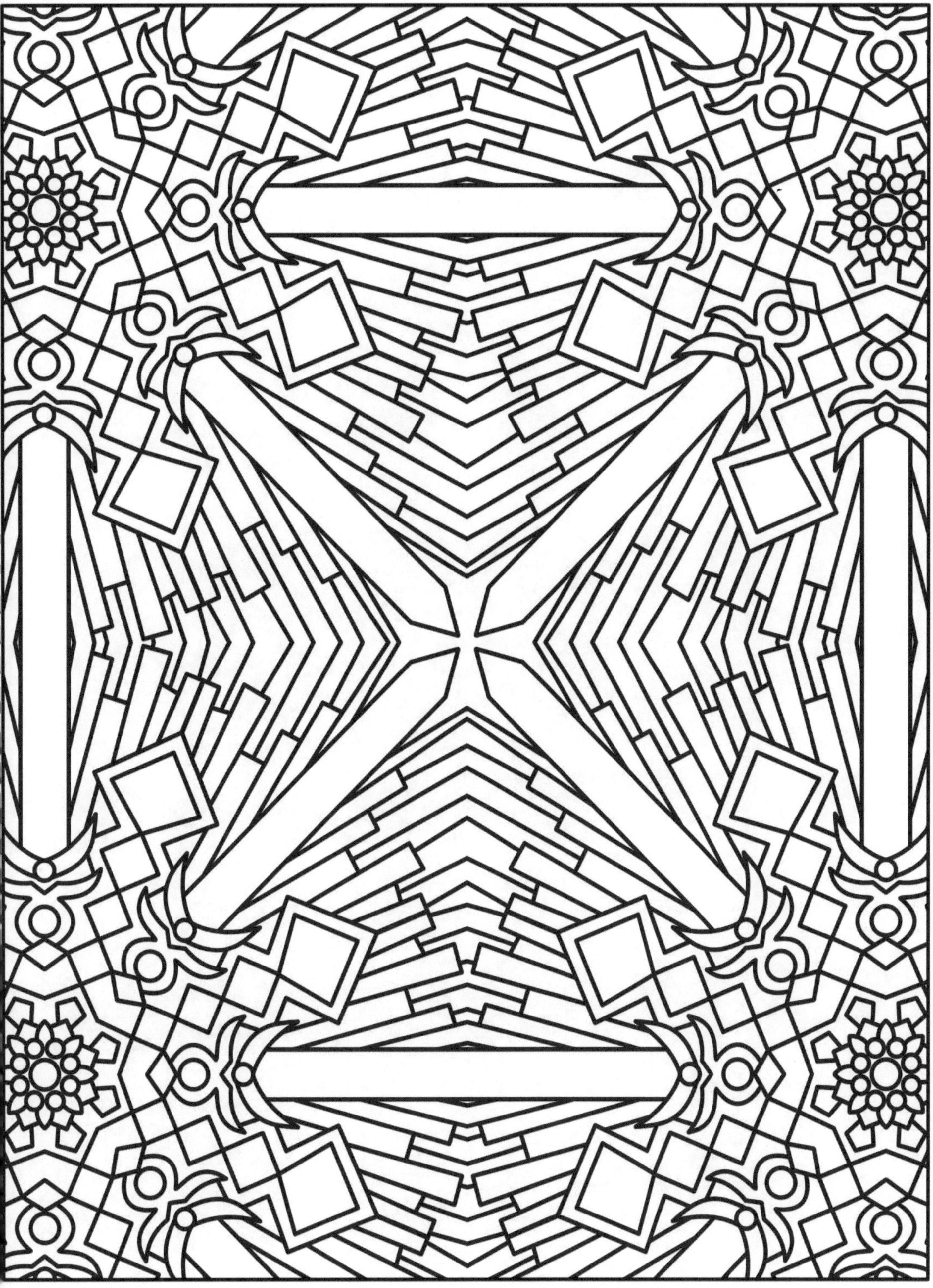

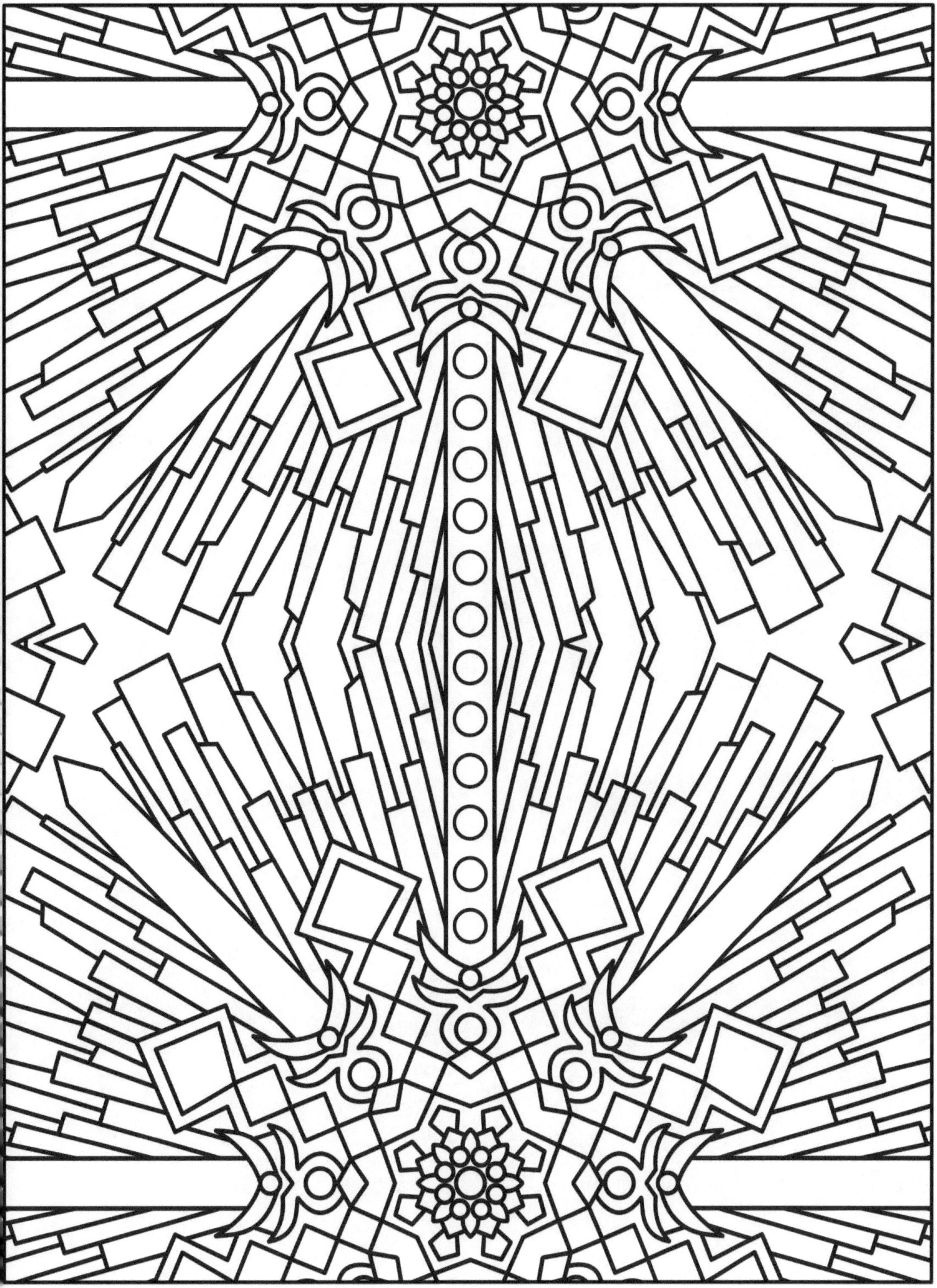

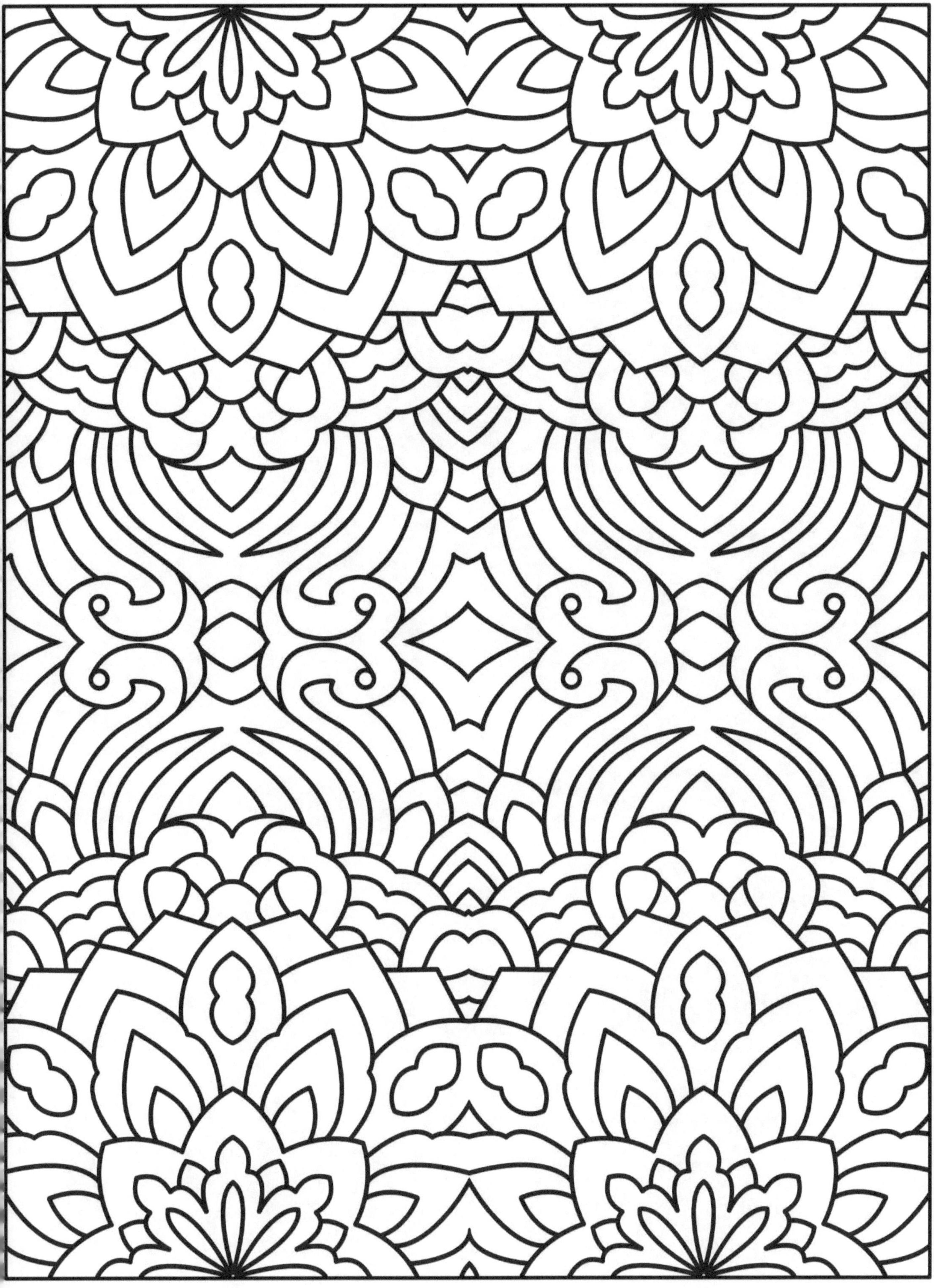

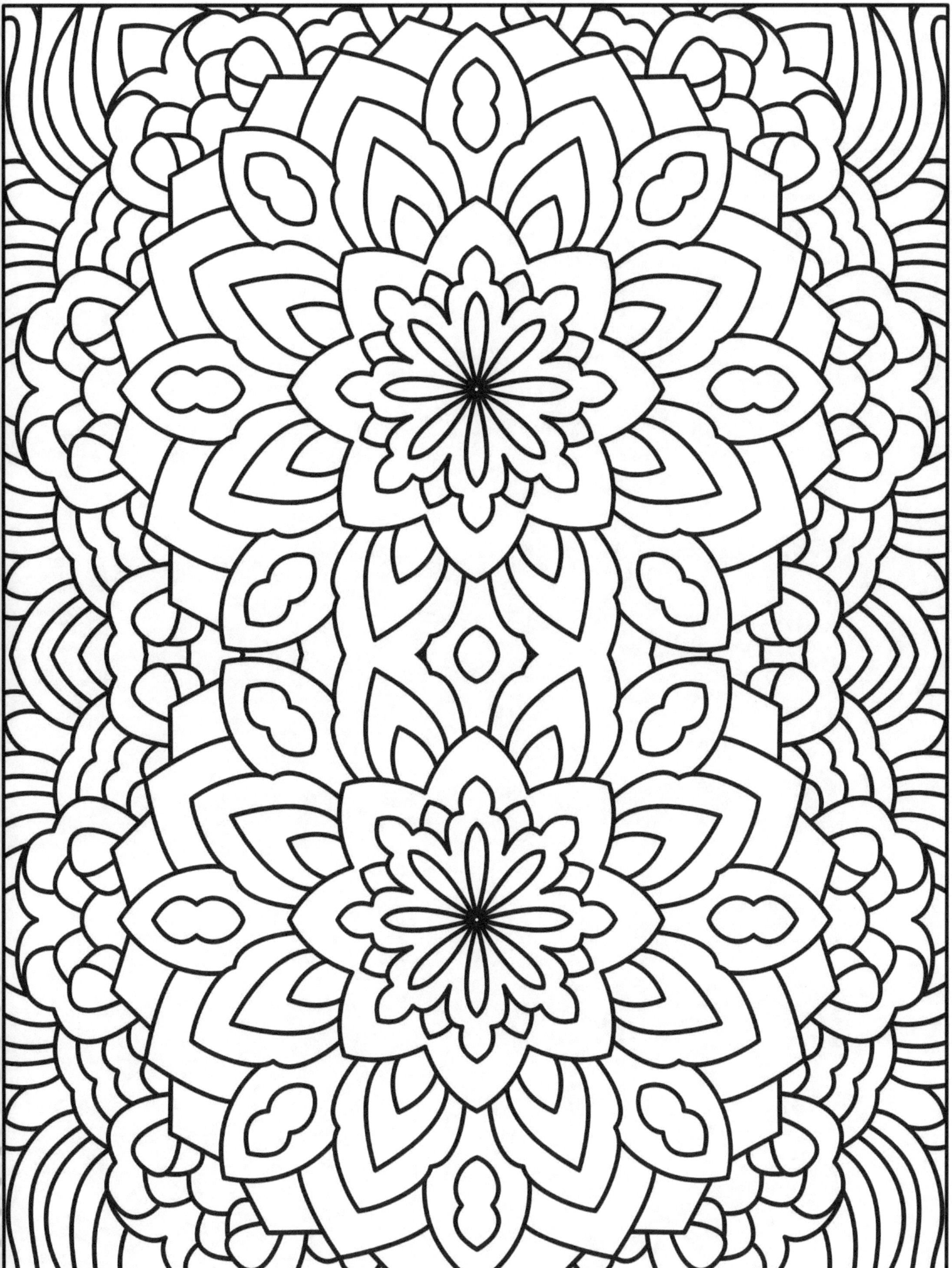

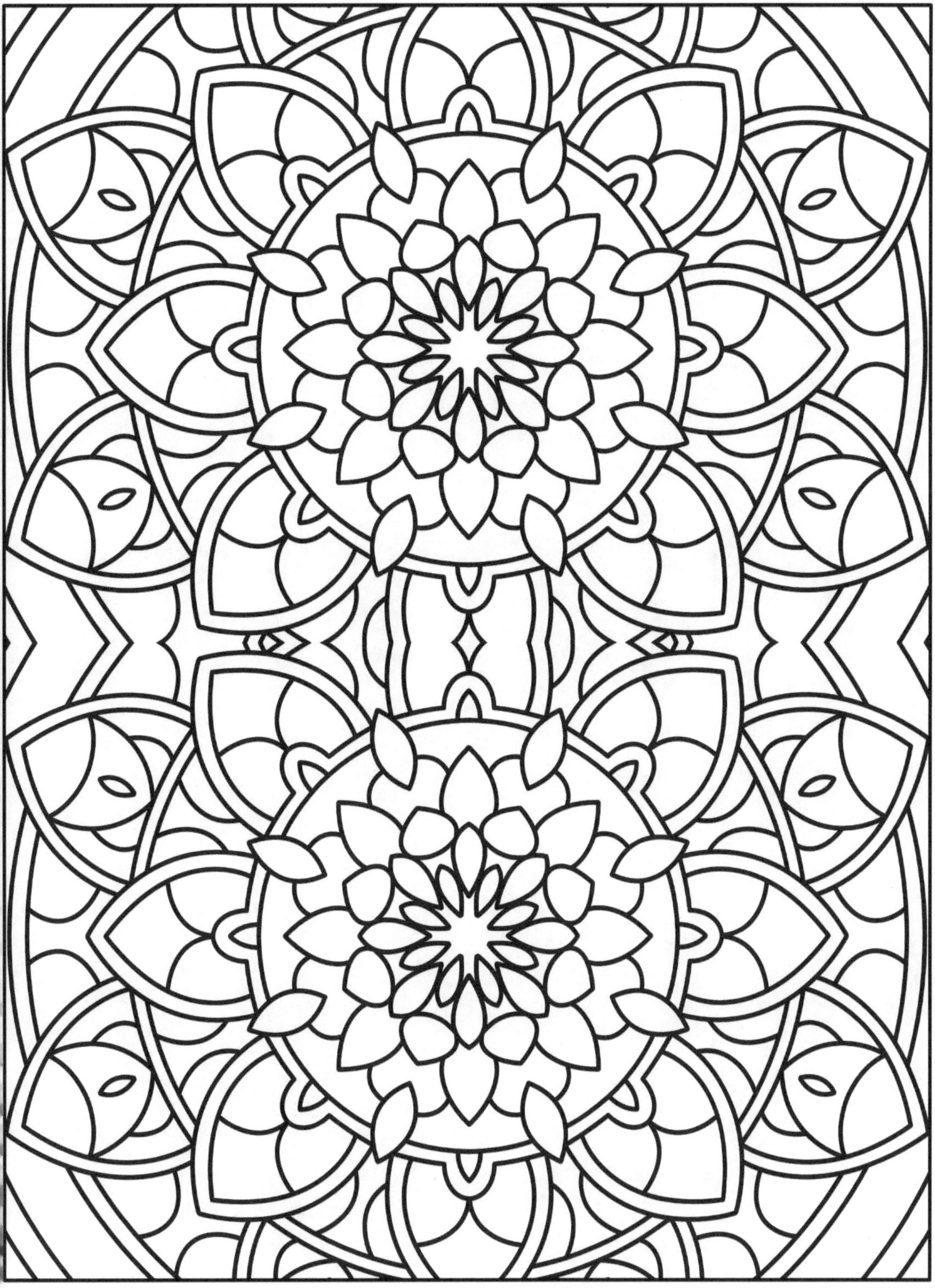

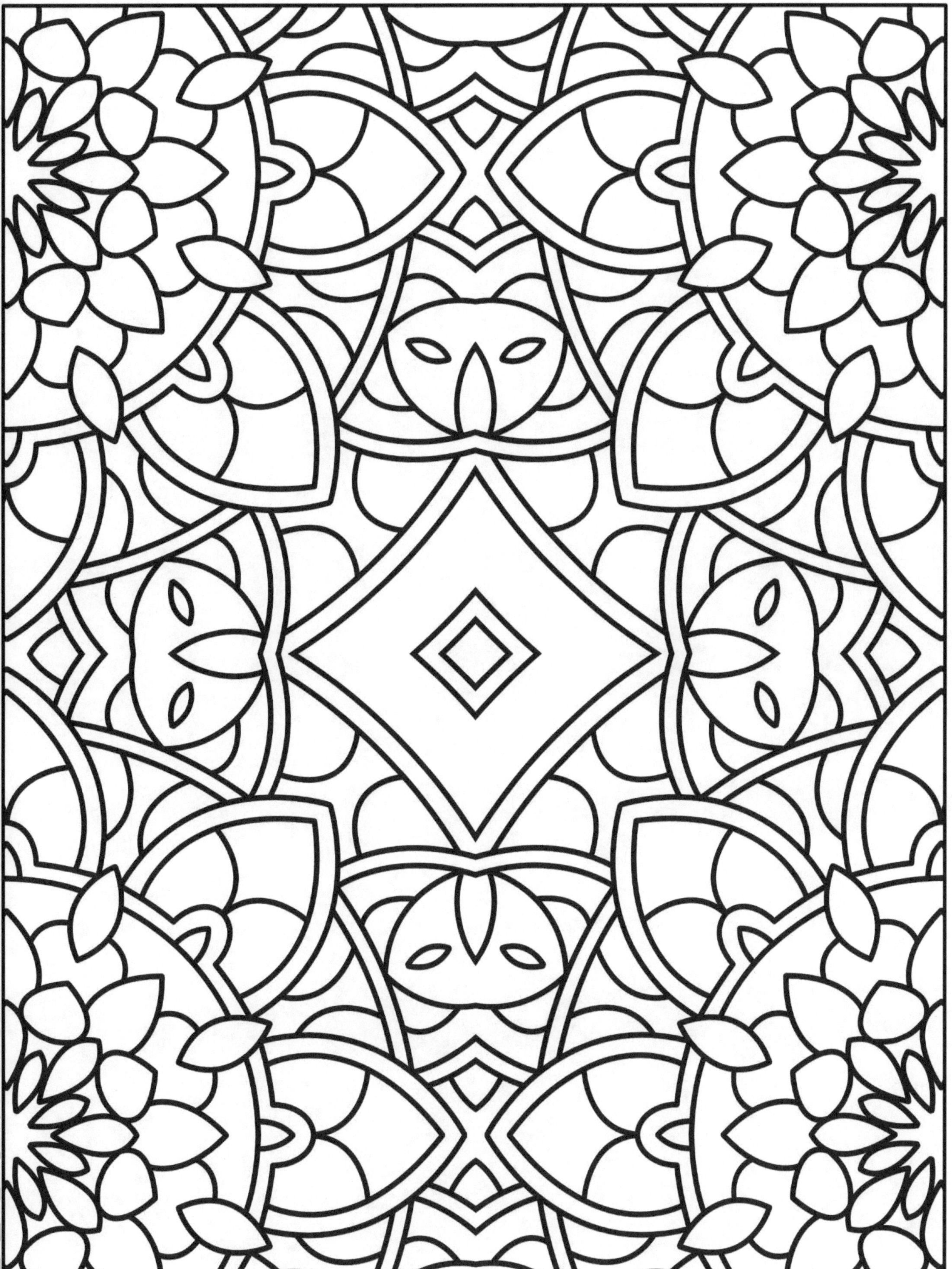

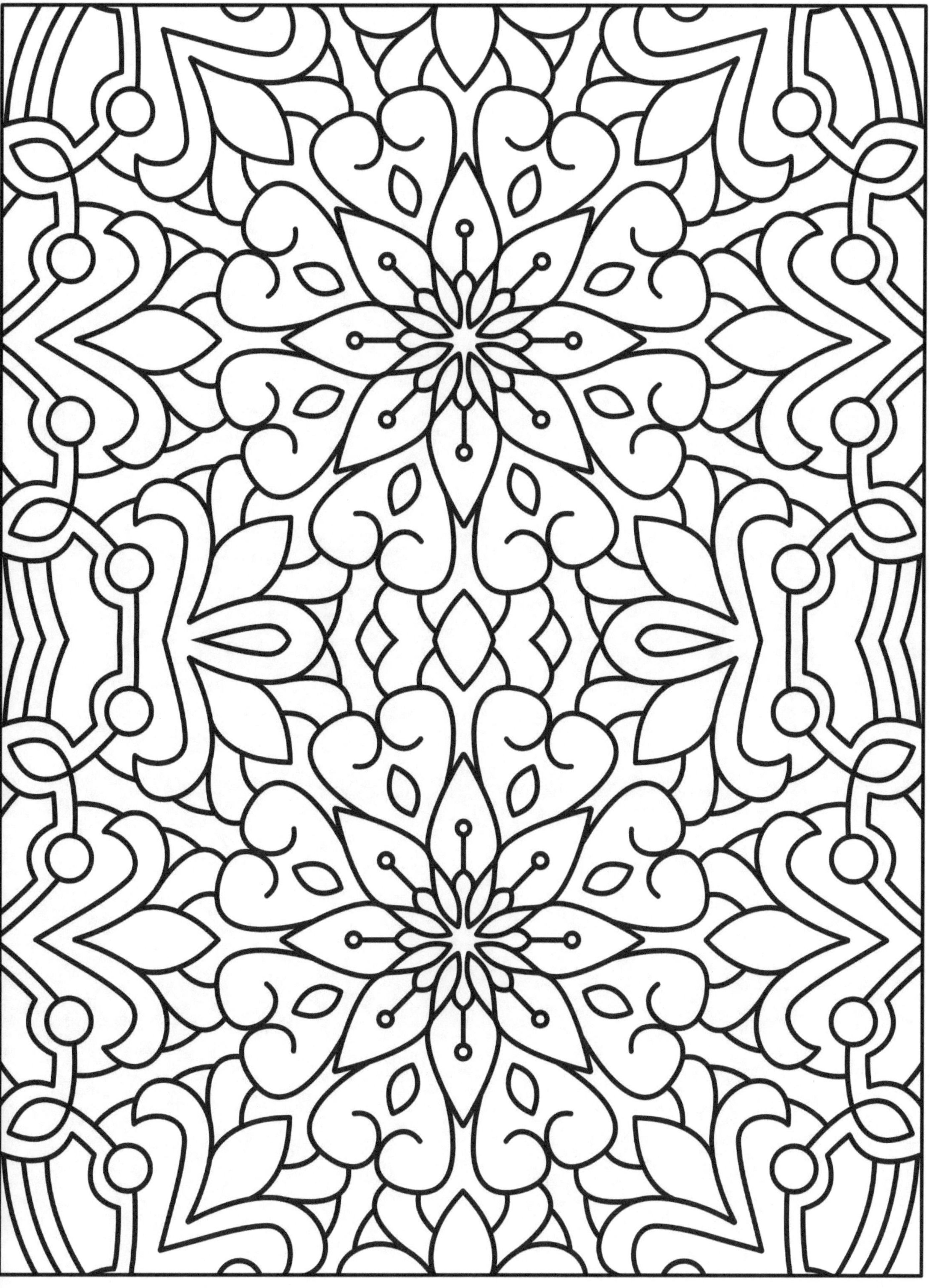

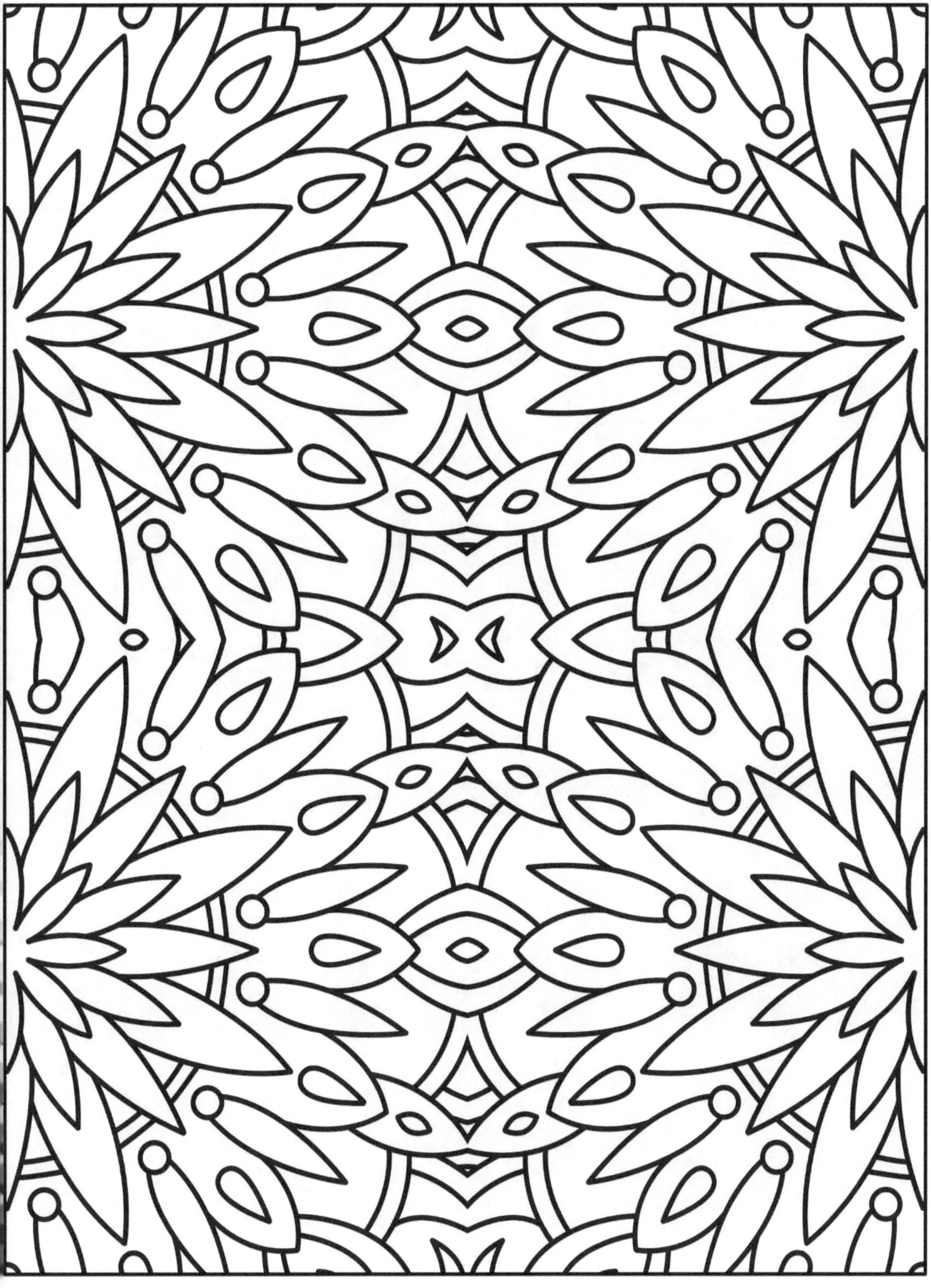

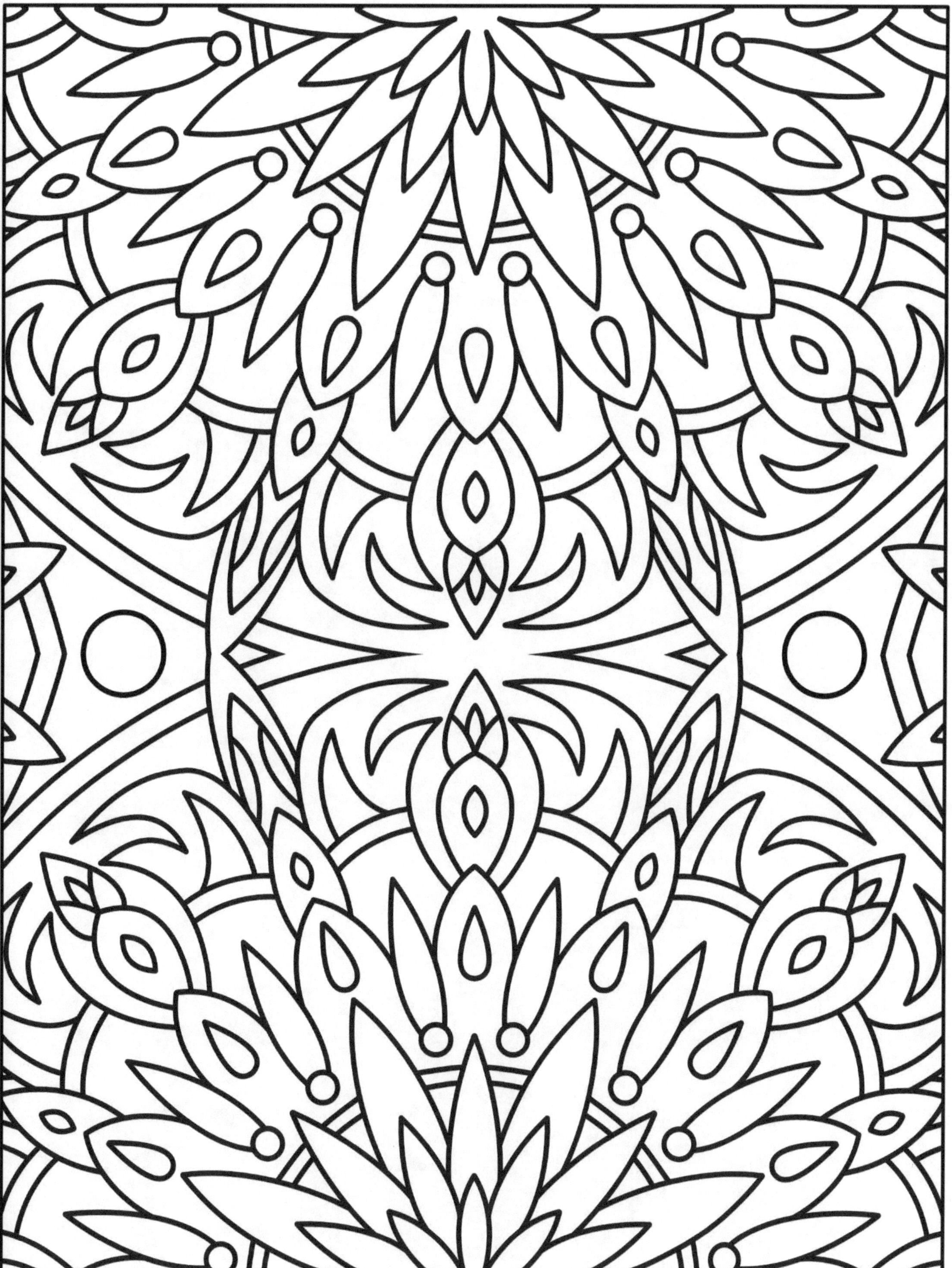

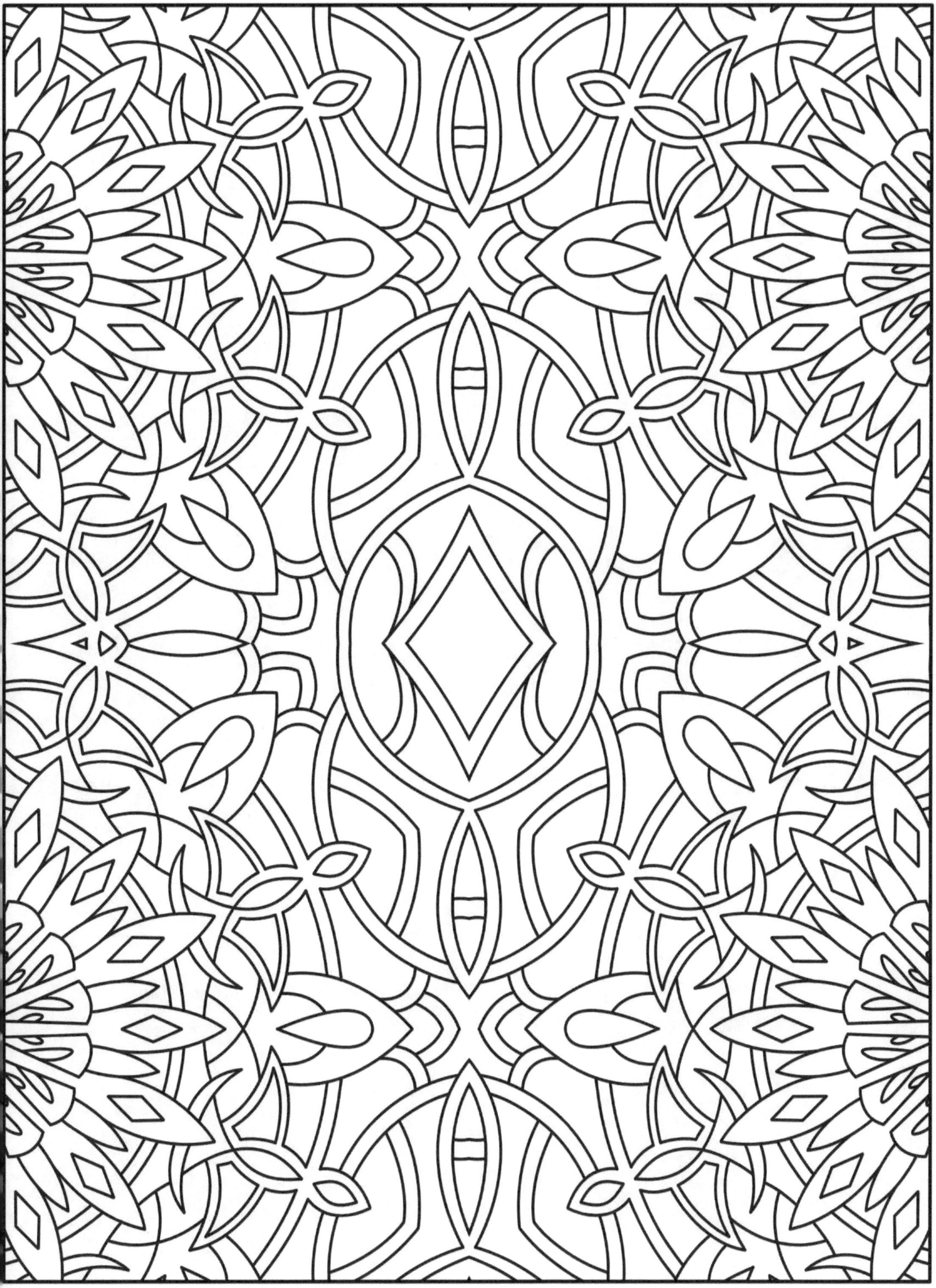

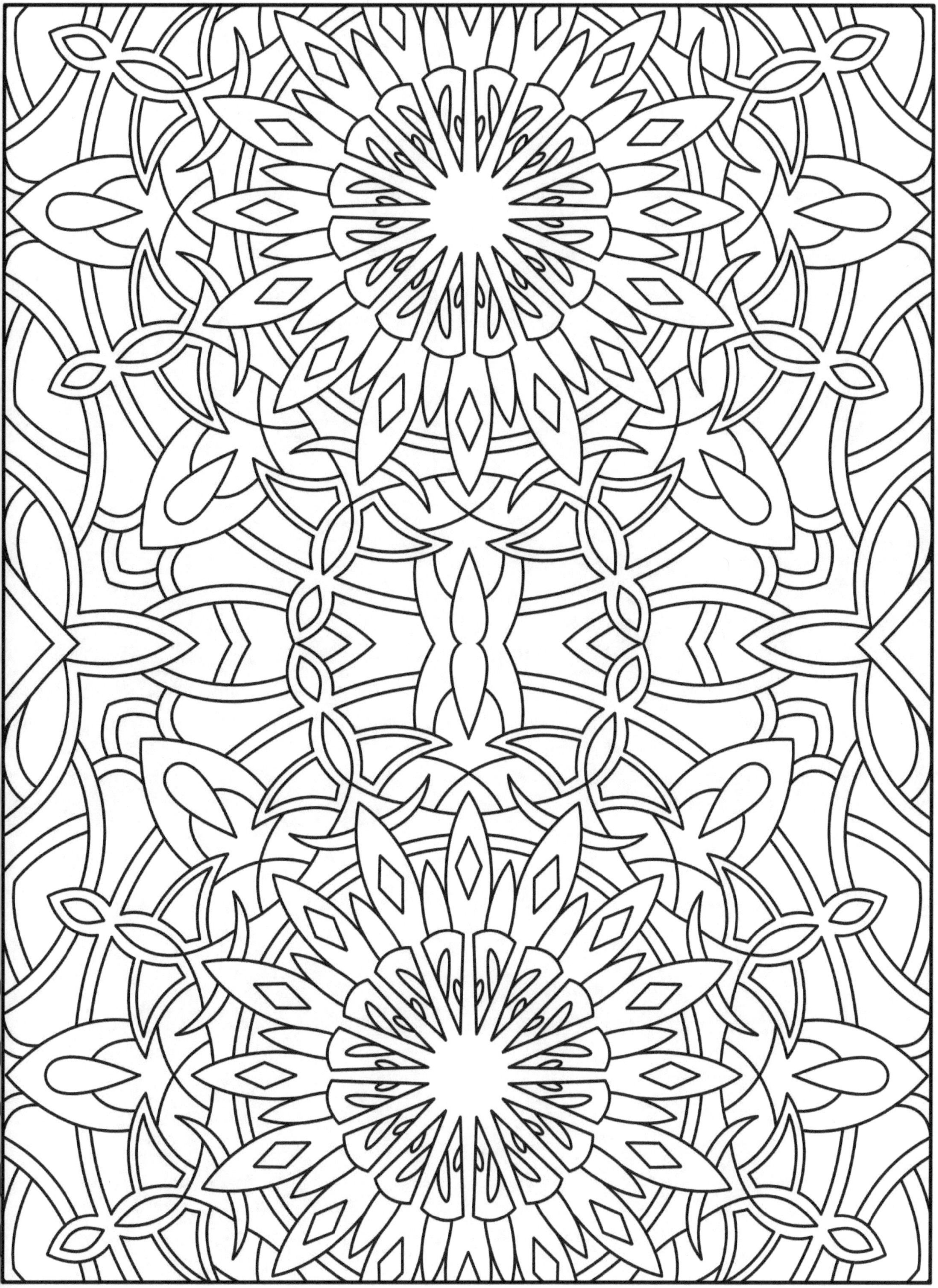

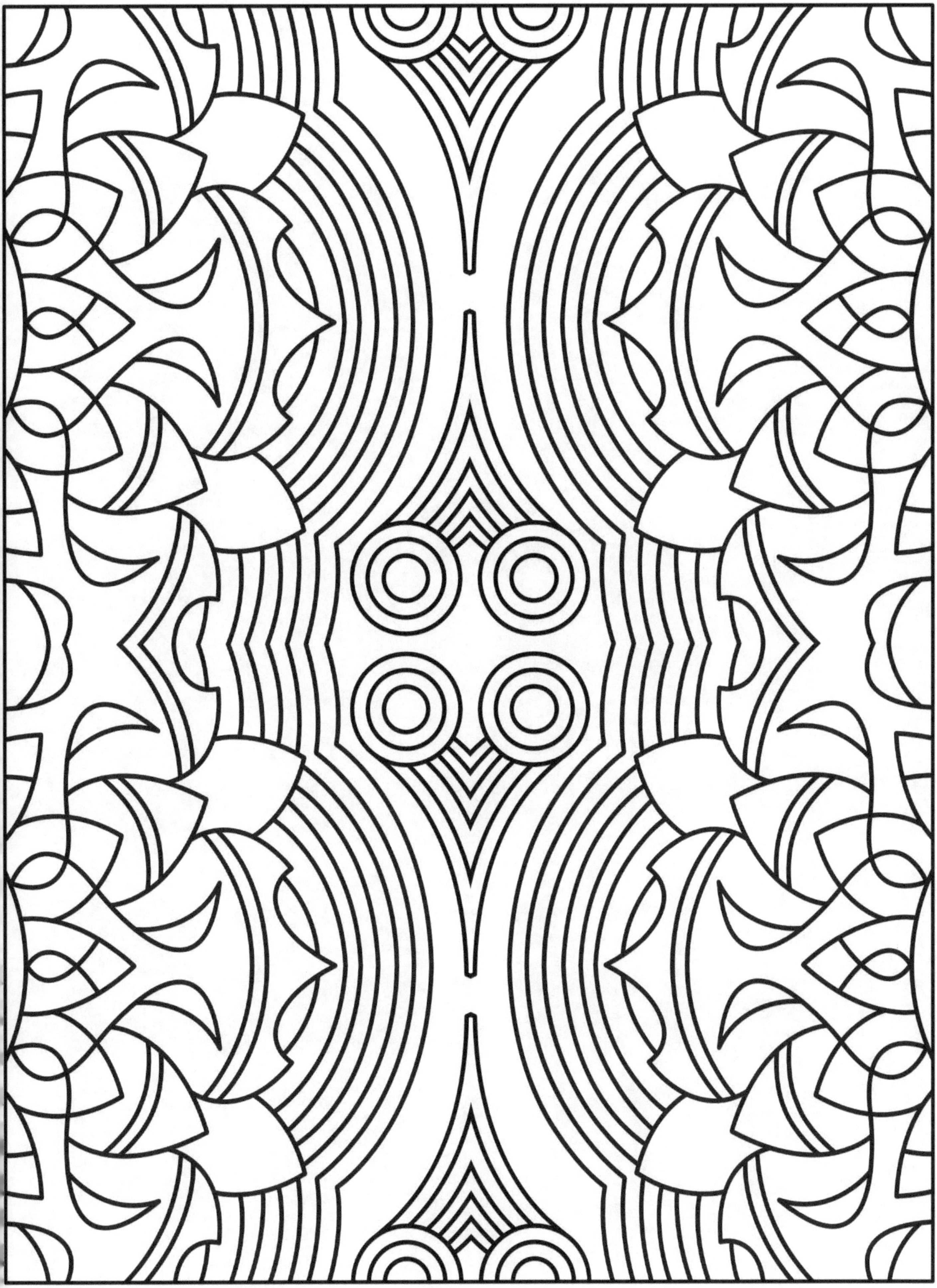

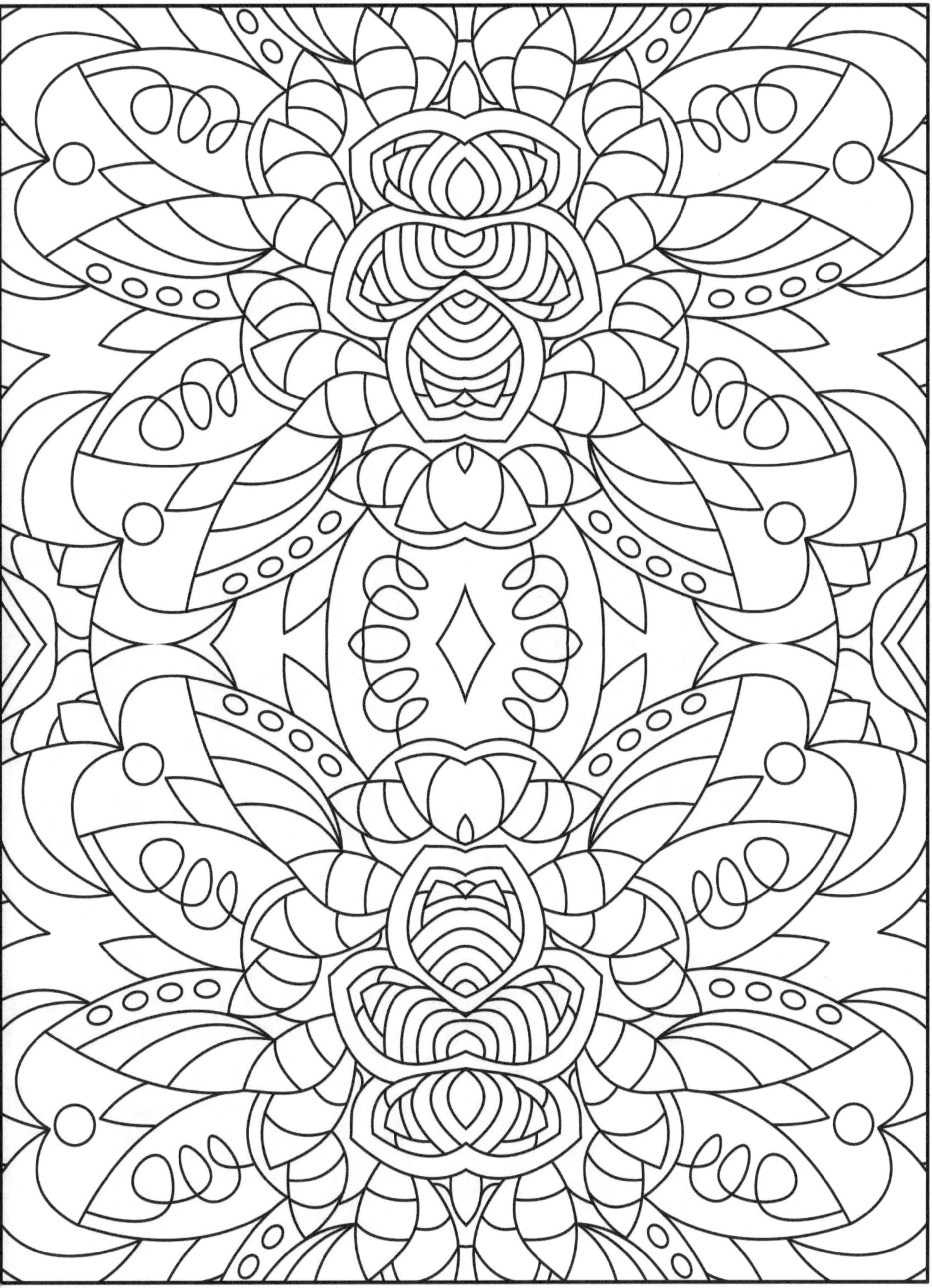

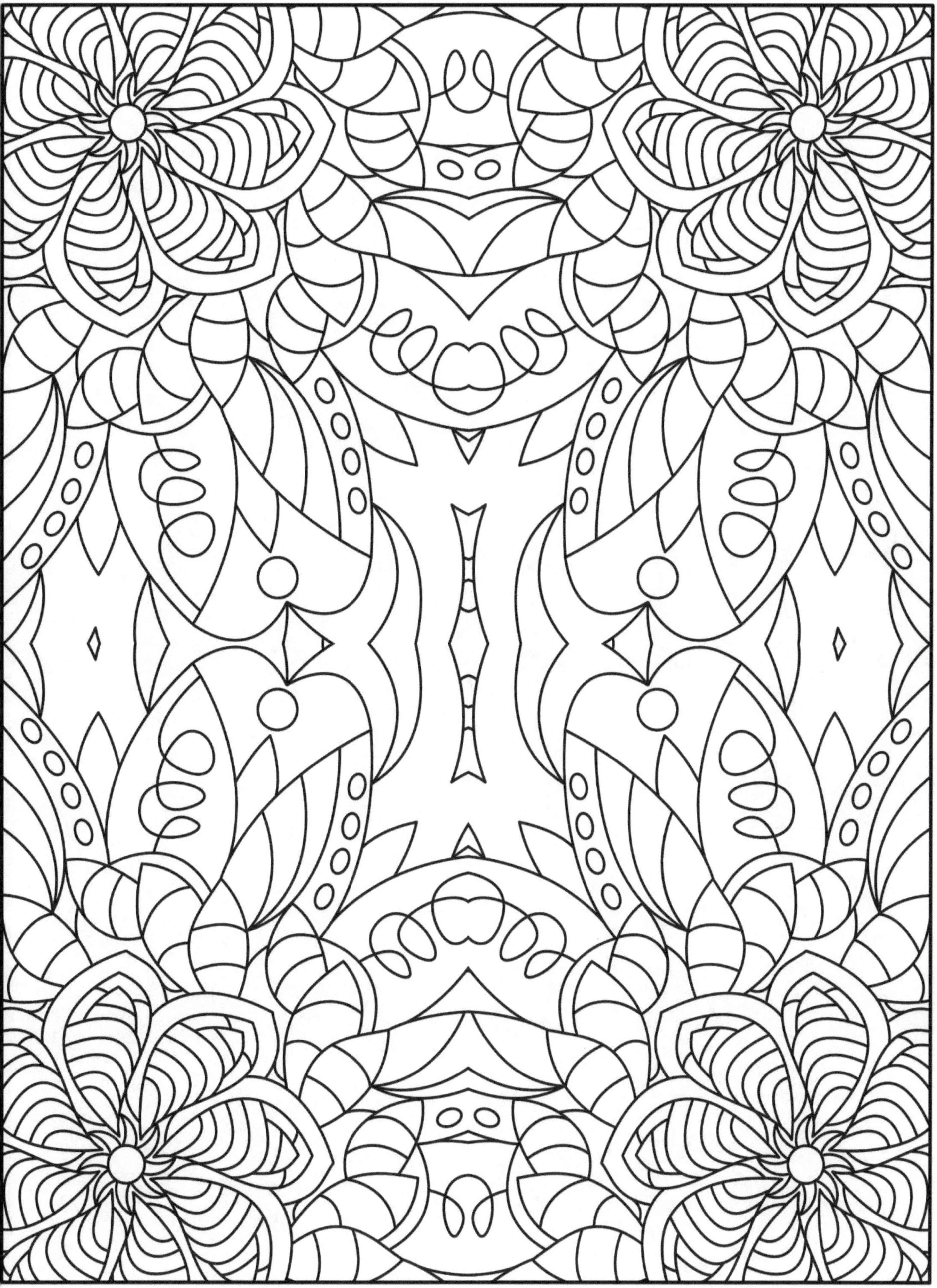

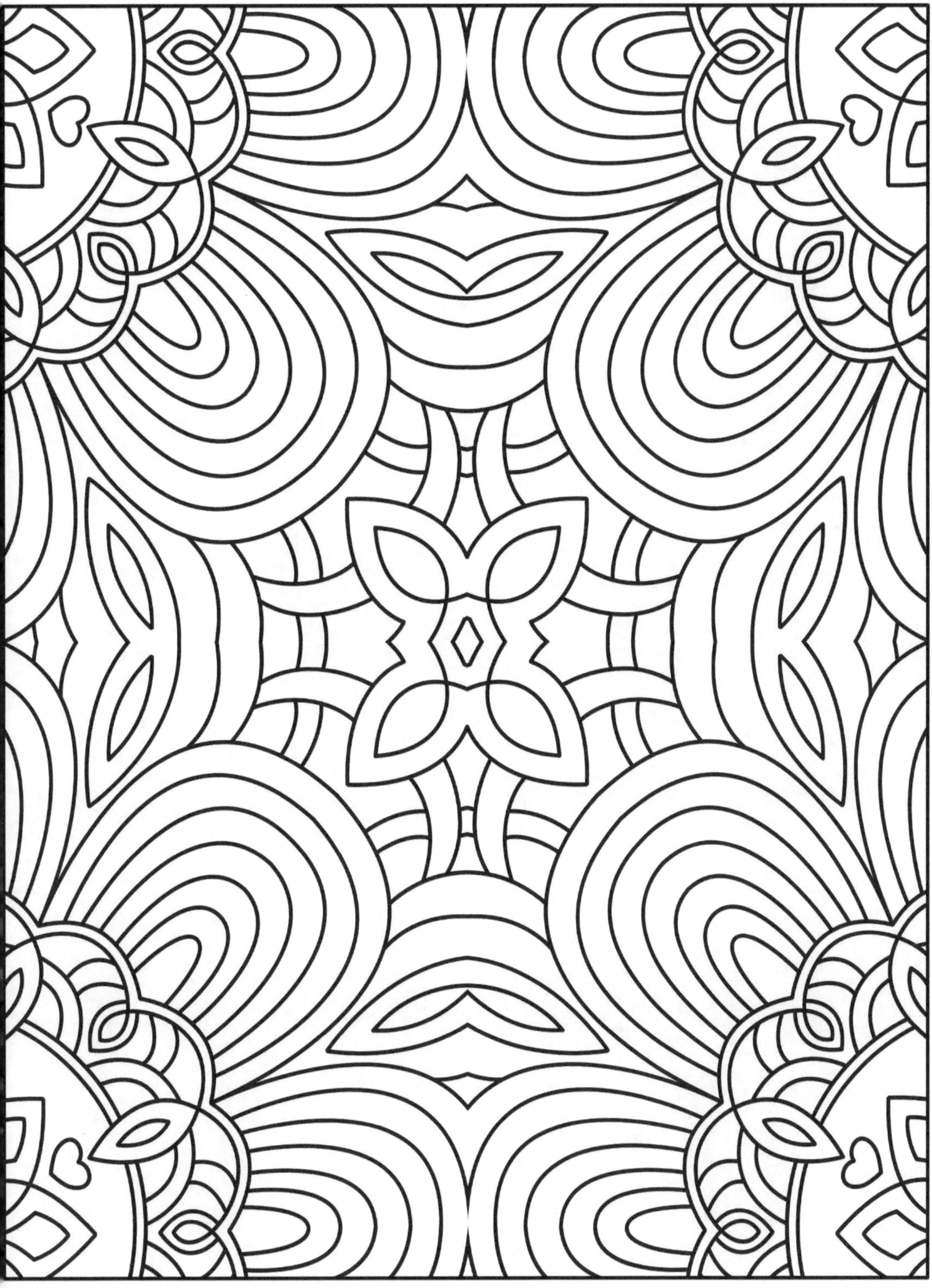

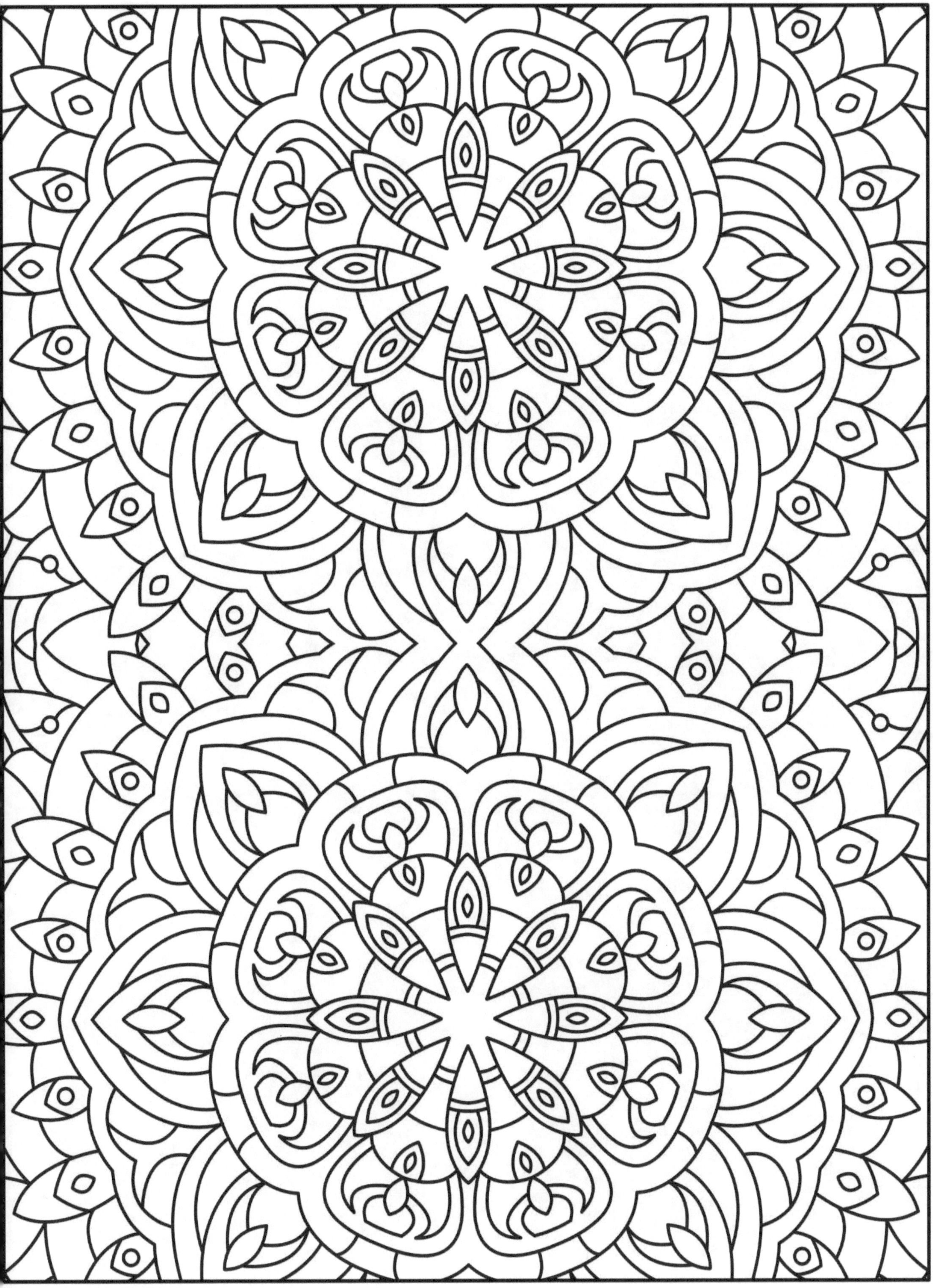

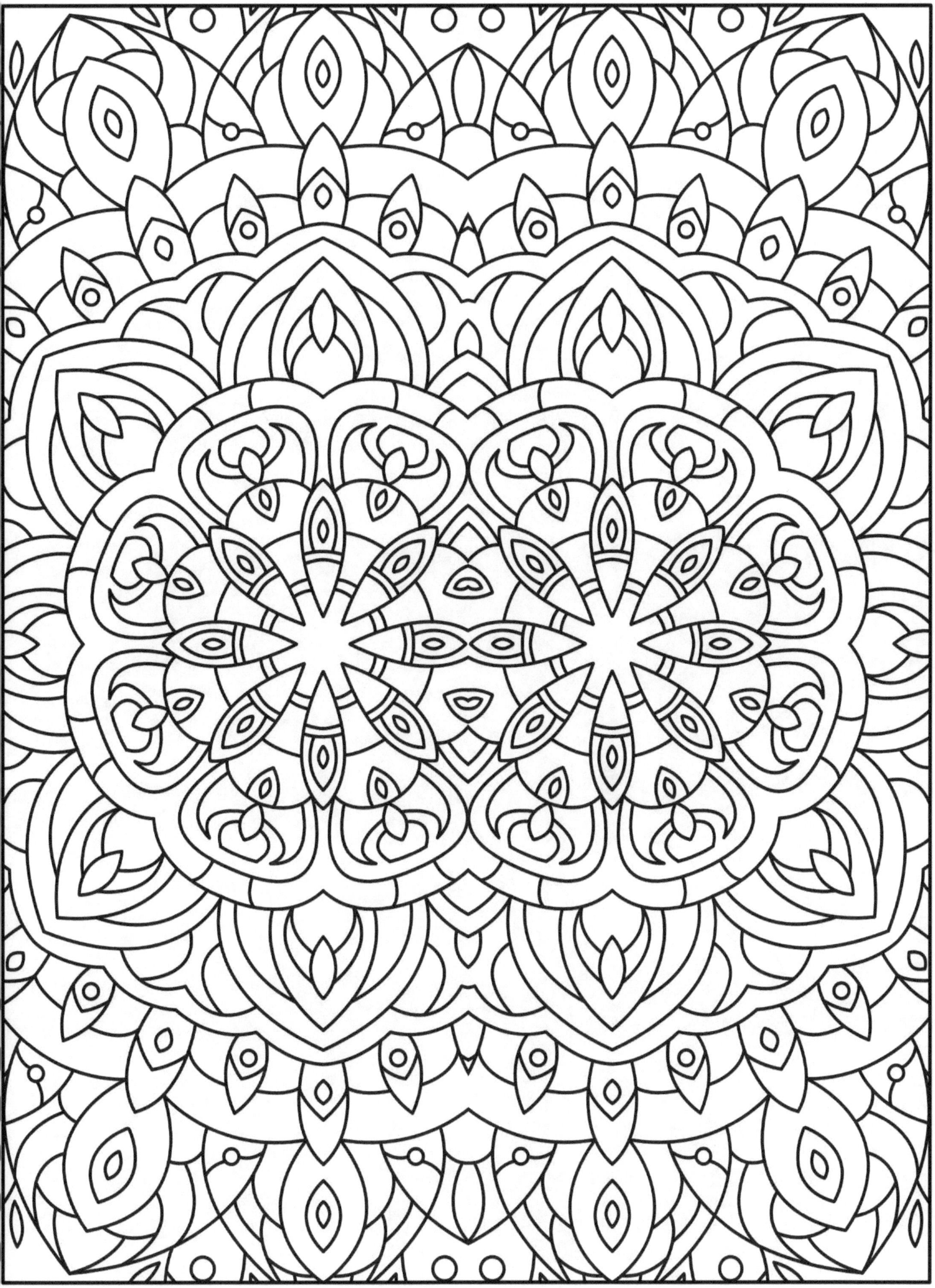

Made in United States
Troutdale, OR
07/18/2023

11374982R00060